ANDRA URSUȚA

ΔΕΣΤΕ

DESTE Foundation for Contemporary Art

ANDRA URSUȚA

2000 WORDS

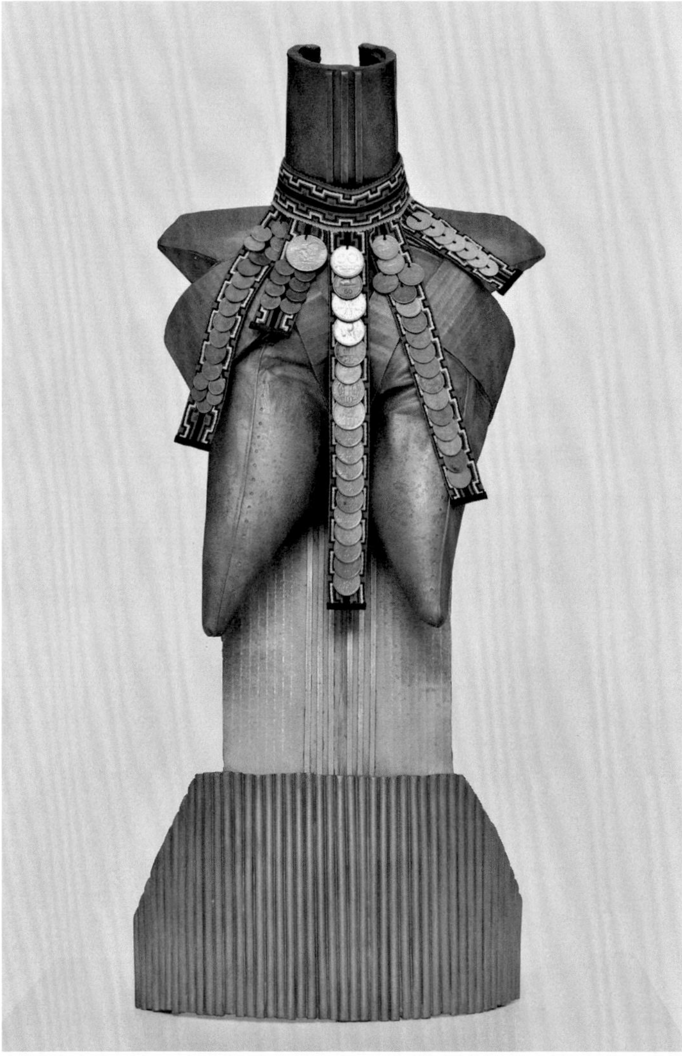

HER DARK MATERIALS

Ali Subotnick

Andra Ursuța's provocative artwork is by turns perverse, absurd, weird, irreverent, visceral, blunt, and melancholic. Ursuța was born in Salonta, Romania (aka Transylvania), and grew up in what she has described as bleak conditions. While it's difficult to fully imagine her upbringing from her own anecdotes and descriptions, Ursuța treats these memories as the inspiration and raw material for her sculptures, drawings, and installations. This is evident in a meticulous and haunting series of dioramas she made of the various rooms in her childhood home (most of the works in this series are titled after the house address: T. Vladimirescu Nr. 5). Each miniature stage set is painstakingly arranged, so accurate and lifelike it could have been zapped by a shrinking machine. Its theatrical nature conjures an immediate empathy, enabling the viewer to experience and examine every detail of the space and evidence of its inhabitants.

The pantry (*T. Vladimirescu Nr. 5, Pantry*, 2013) features diminutive replicas of a stepladder, a stool, a rake, a mini refrigerator, a bucket, a shovel, and a table with glasses and pitchers. The kitchen (*T. Vladimirescu Nr. 5, Kitchen*, 2013) contains light green cabinets and tables, jars, a meat grinder, and a tipped-over stool, while the bedroom (*T. Vladimirescu Nr. 5, Sleeping*

Room, 2013) includes true-to-life tiny facsimiles of floor rugs and a wall tapestry. Most haunting is the "nutria room" (*Lucian*, 2014), a dank space with a brick wall, one side window, and a stark cement floor, largely empty except for a plastic carboy (a type of container generally used to hold hazardous liquids) and an empty noose hanging from the ceiling. Knowing that this is where the nutrias were shorn gives this particular room a dark weight (Ursuța's family raised nutrias, a rat- or beaver-like animal, whose fur has been harvested for fashion since the 1930s). And knowing it's the room where her uncle hung himself intensifies the gloom. These haunted spaces clearly originate out of a deep personal connection and history. Yet, for all its melancholy, Ursuța's work is infused with a strangely matter-of-fact attitude. There's no woe-is-me martyrdom. Rather, it's fierce, proud, gut-punching work, confronting basic human issues—fear, death, memory, identity, and more.

Not all of Ursuța's work is so dark or so personal—humor abounds throughout—but she does approach every project with a frankness that is hardly typical among contemporary artists. Drawing from her personal history, memories, and phobias, as well as the mass media and news—fake, real, alternative—she concocts ridiculous situations and absurdly humorous objects. For two witty sculptures, Ursuța adopted unlikely materials—for *Toiletpaper Stove* (2008) she carved the sculpture inside a roll of toilet paper, and with *Souvenir Salami/ Family Portrait* (2008) she painted a family portrait directly onto the exposed side of a log of salami. For a 2012 exhibition, Ursuța crammed forty-two multicolored polyurethane stools made from a cast of her upturned rear end into her gallery's storage space (each stool bears a unique title, like *Backstabber*, *Frostitute*, and *Sister Swallow*, all 2012). Poking fun at the dicks women must wrestle with in order to achieve success (among other things), she created a climbing wall with dildos in place of rocks and grips (*Alps*, 2016). For a series of obelisk sculptures, Ursuța transformed the phallic and staid symbol of triumph into a playful, cartoonish figure, everything but monumental and reverent.

These anthropomorphized objects, replete with orifices and protrusions, sit on chairs (both *Untitled*, 2015, pp. 61–73) like attentive audience members. Experimenting with both material and form, Ursuța combines ingredients like an alchemist, exploiting materials and their limitations, and adopting some for "off-label" use. This is apparent in the obelisks and other sculptures that Ursuța fabricated from resin and filled with produce, resembling a 1970s Jell-O casserole or objects trapped in amber. She's clearly having a laugh at our obsessions and preoccupations.

Laughter, sadness, and repulsion share equal billing in Ursuța's work, and this approach mitigates the artist's distressing subject matter without resorting to overt sentimentality or clichés. She documents trauma and tragedy, working through her own phobias in the process. Inspired by an ironic news story describing a group of Gypsy witches who put a curse on the Romanian government to protest a law recognizing witchcraft as a legitimate and taxable occupation, Ursuța's 2012 exhibition *Magical Terrorism* at Ramiken Crucible in New York imagined these witches as heroic women, hybrids of several cultures. Occupying a vandalized gallery space (she broke the front windows) was Ursuța's sculptural interpretation of the activist Gypsy witches.

Conversion Table (2014, p. 37), a striking copper bust, features sagging breasts, a torso striated like a piece of corrugated cardboard, and a pipe-like neck with strands of coins hanging from a fabric choker. The piece brings together multiple references, from African art to Roman classicism and European modernism—a Venus de Milo from an alternate universe. Adding another layer to this story, three identical marble figures, all titled *Commerce Exterieur Mondial Sentimental* (2012/2017, pp. 75–83), were inspired by a photograph Ursuța found on a news site documenting an unknown Romanian Gypsy awaiting deportation. Layering reference and meaning, appropriating cultural artifacts and physical attributes, Ursuța creates an alternate universe of victims and heroes, saviors and criminals.

In addition to drawing inspiration from personal memories and news media, Ursuța often references the folklore of her homeland. The irreverent *Ass to Mouth* (2010), a wooden stake soaked in iodine, is a scaled-down replica of the Romanian artist Constantin Brancusi's *Endless Column* (1918), which was a tribute to Romanian soldiers who died fighting Germany in World War I, as well as a reference to Vlad the Impaler (aka Dracula), Transylvania's most notorious antihero. Ursuța twists things even further by covering the stake's surface with black rubber rhomboid modules, turning it into an S&M fetish object and thereby both eroticizing the act of impalement and defiling Brancusi's modernist masterpiece. In a similar vein, her reimagined household mops (both titled *Floor Licker*, 2013, pp. 21–23) feature engorged, bruised, oversize tongues in place of mop heads. The familiar object distorted by this grotesque tongue evokes befuddlement and disgust, while conjuring a severe form of punishment or fetishism—to lick the floor clean. This pairing of a monstrous tongue with an everyday mop handle shifts back and forth between real and surreal, repulsive and funny, functional and useless. Like *Ass to Mouth*, her untitled series of weaponry formed out of bicycle parts and metal are at once threatening and formally considered, a Duchampian pun with violent potential (*Untitled*, 2014, pp. 32–33).

Ursuța's sick humor continues with *CruciFritz* (2014, p. 35), in which the artist cast a toy version of the *Bundesadler*, the double-headed black eagle of Germany's coat of arms, dating back to the Weimar Republic and later adopted as a symbol for the Nazi Party. The grave image, infamous in its unadulterated state, was first transformed into an impotent inflatable toy, then cast in a light green–colored concrete. A weightless object rendered heavy; a weighty symbol rendered inert. Another cast of an inflatable toy, *Summer Kampf* (2015, pp. 53–55), expands on Ursuța's twisted jokes about the Holocaust and other traumatic historical events by turning a raft into a concrete female torso with deflated breasts. For *Atrophy Room* (2015, pp. 39–47), the artist hung terra-cotta jugs at various heights on the walls. As the title suggests, she's crafted a trophy wall, but instead of the taxidermies of hunted prey, she celebrates a common object, lifeless and functionless.

Ursuța's explorations of technique and material, pain and discomfort don't overshadow her artistic strengths. She can draw, sculpt, and otherwise craft images and objects that are poetic, beautiful, captivating, and hypnotic, as demonstrated by a series of photograms on velvet. The subdued and cheeky *Guarda Che Luna* (2015, p. 49) features two arms holding a pole from which an oversize carrot dangles. Pavlov's classical conditioning metaphor—his ultimate tease—becomes a ghostly image. Painted with Optium on velvet and canvas, it's a prime example of Ursuța's indifference to traditional material uses. Another work in the series, *Slavesitting* (2015, pp. 50–51), depicts a minotaur casually sitting atop a masked man on all fours. *Tomatopig* (2015, pp. 57–59) is made from dyed velvet and imagines its title—a pig-like creature, floating in a moonlit sky. Each piece in the series is set within a handmade wooden frame, deepening the sense of intimacy.

In her large-scale sculptures and installations, Ursuța utilizes a similar strategy of creating charged situations and objects, and merging corporeal and emotional affect. With *Orthodoctrinator* (2014, pp. 24–31), a complex piece inspired by a church the artist saw in a small Romanian airport, Ursuța crafted a brainwashing machine of sorts—five shingled spires sprout from a contraption of crumbling brick walls and painted aluminum siding, mashed together like a makeshift shed in a shantytown. The backside reveals a mechanism for the spires, with dangling wires and light fixtures attached to deteriorating tiles. At the base of each spire is a helmet-like element, like old-fashioned hair dryers attached to the back of salon chairs. Reminiscent of a torture device, the work and its title evoke the horror of mass indoctrination, seeming to suggest it's something we should still fear.

Obsessiveness and intensity pervade everything Ursuța does. Her series *The Man from the Internet* (2007–2017) includes 100 ink drawings depicting the decaying corpse of a victim of the Russian-Chechen conflicts in the 1990s, later unearthed from a mass grave. Ursuța first saw the image on an unofficial Russian-English news website that is no longer online, and throughout the past decade she has continued to draw this image in meticulous detail. As time passed and the artist continued to revisit and reinterpret this haunting image, political events altered the landscape of the post-Soviet world, and the online world grew and transformed at an accelerated rate. Yet for Ursuța, time almost stood still: that man was still dead, his corpse still rotting, his identity still unknown. The enigmatic nature of the image's source mirrors the mystery of the figure's identity and the circumstances of his death. With each drawing, Ursuța faces off with the inevitability of death, man's struggle against man, unending chaos, violence, and disaster. Considering all 100 drawings together, the horror of the image begins to subside, and the sensitivity and careful attention within each drawing surpasses the sense of despondence.

The artist is not immune to her own machinations. Fear of death—a subject she says she thinks about constantly—is a key theme in her work. In the self-portrait sculpture *Crush* (2011), the artist has been mummified and covered in semen. The piece was partly inspired by a news item about a young Romanian man who flew to London hidden in the wheel compartment of a plane. The story appeared just a few years ago, long after the fall of the Iron Curtain and at a time when Romanians were permitted to travel to England without a visa. The man in the story was born after the collapse of Communism, and Ursuța saw his act as “a reflexive gesture of escape, maybe passed down through cultural memory, that was perpetuated endlessly, long after the interdictions that made escape attempts meaningful had ended.” The title of the work refers to a love crush, in which the figure of the artist has fallen in love so hard that she is crushed to death. Ursuța says, “The idea is that over a lifetime of ‘crushes,’ and the sex they presumably lead to, a sort of ideal sum of spilled semen flattens the recipient.”

Ursuța’s recurring themes and subjects—memory, death, the human condition, and the farcicality and irony of life—are arguably all the more relevant in today’s unstable political and social climate. Her work is ripe with emotion and contradiction, pathos and drollery, melancholy and hope; it’s raw and refined, hard and soft, aggressive and tender. At once vulgar and political, poignant and wry, exotic and familiar. Downplaying her sharp intuition and intelligence, Ursuța likens herself to “a village idiot who gets prescribed behavior wrong and, in perverting it, undermines the authority that commands it.” A refreshingly honest and original voice, she sees through the bullshit and gets straight to the point, tackling real-world issues, imbued with a dash of existentialism and a bitingly black sense of humor.

All quotations are from telephone conversations and email correspondence with the artist in 2013 and 2014.

WORKS

Floor Licker, 2013

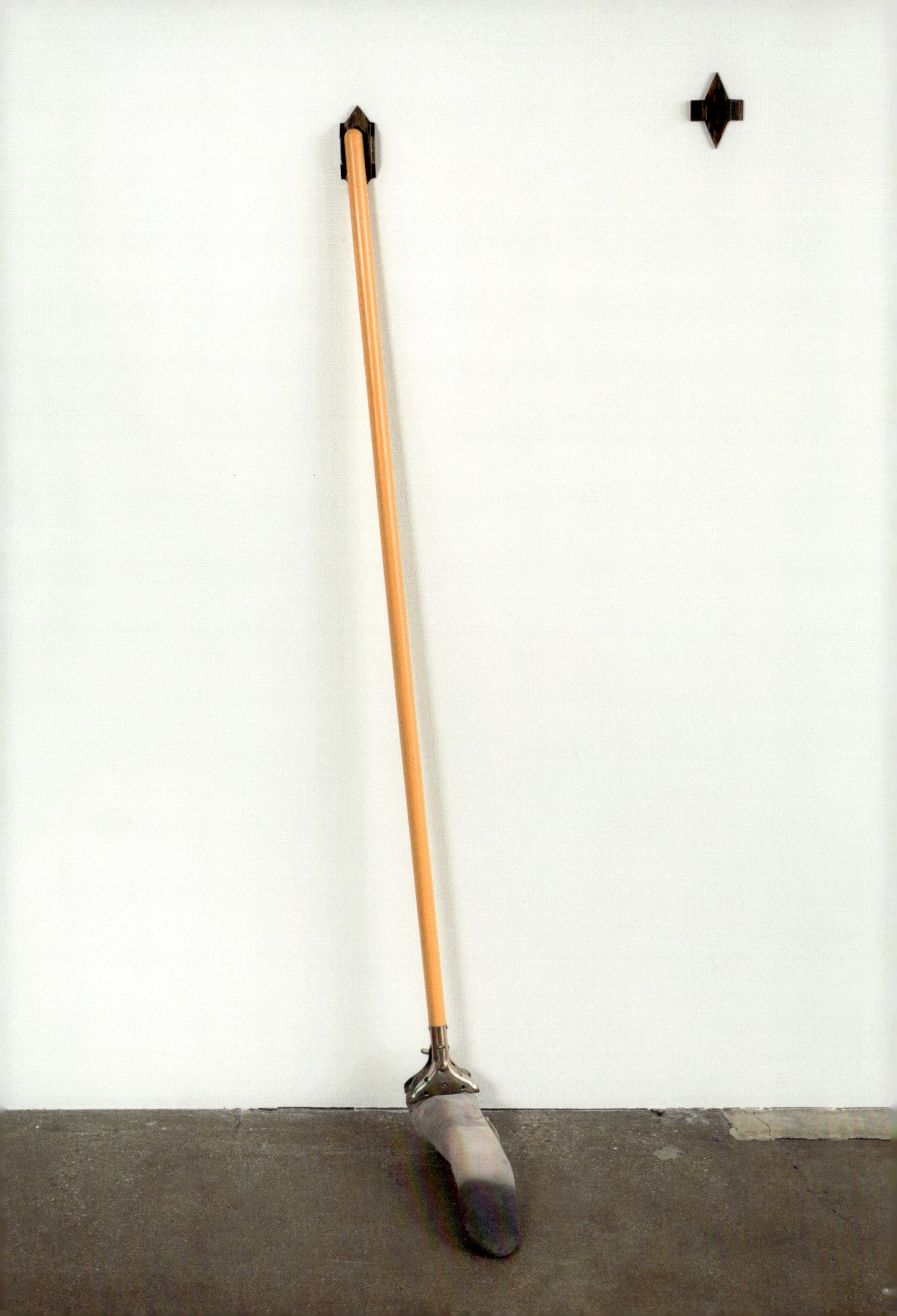

Floor Licker, 2013

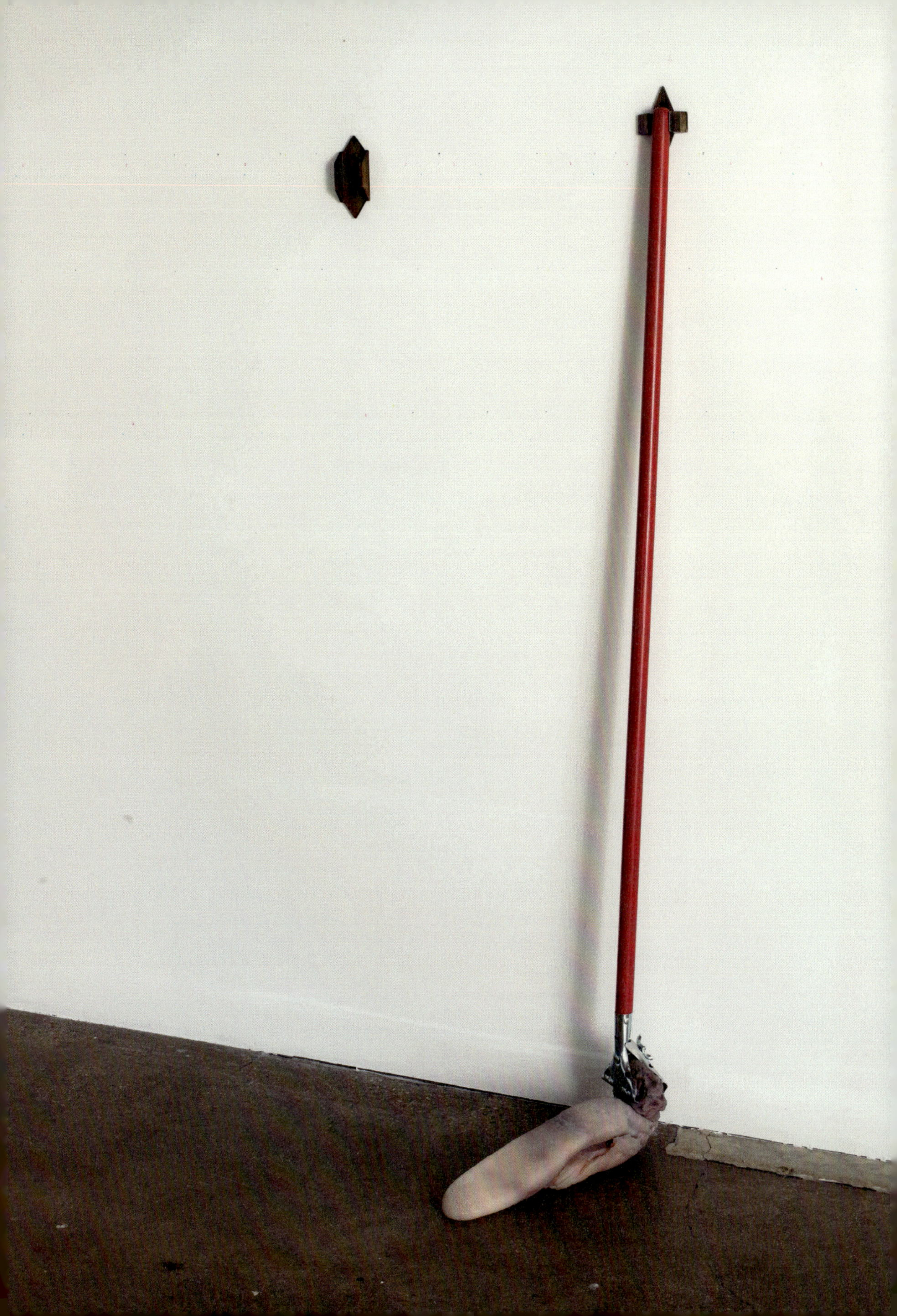

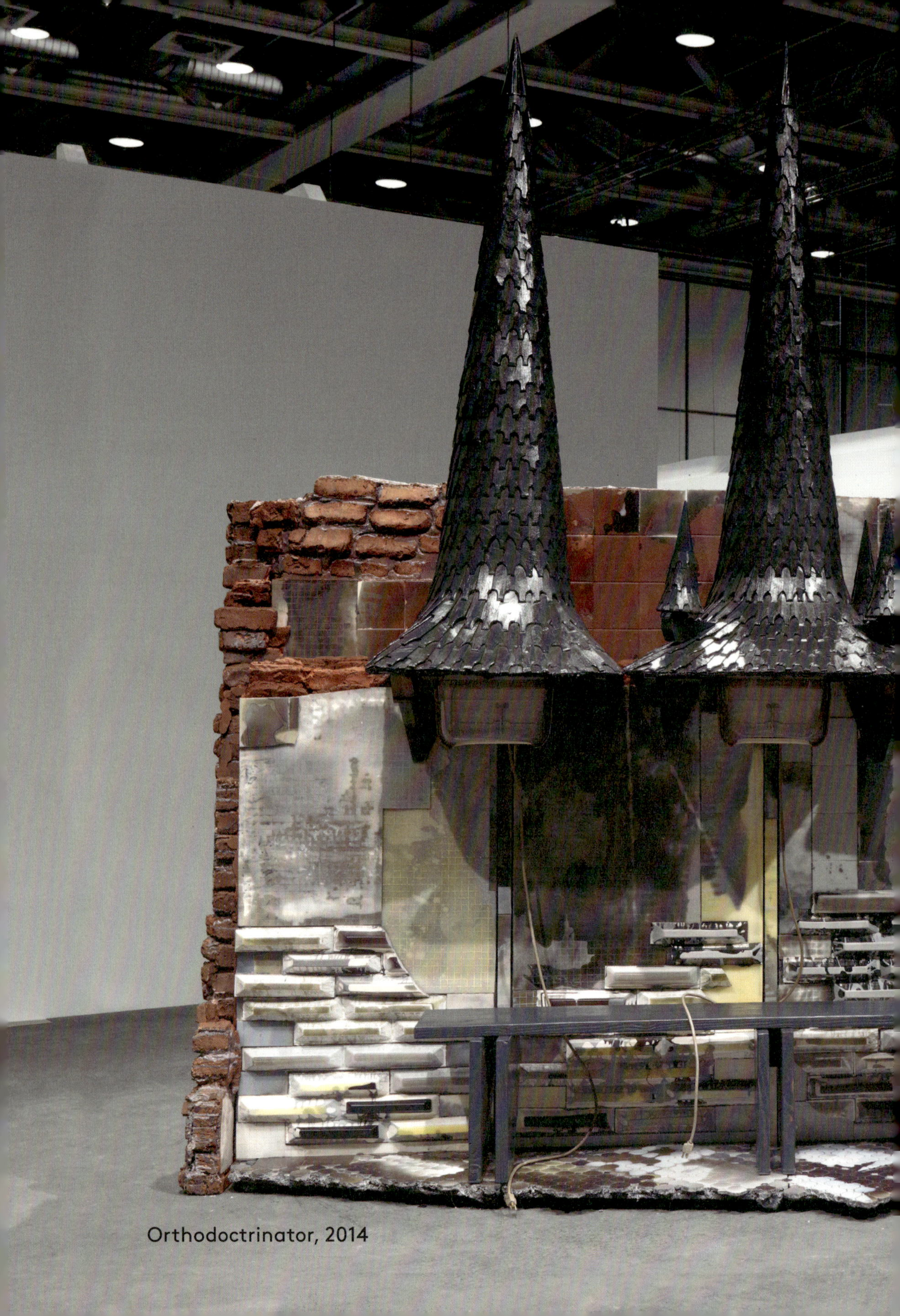

Orthodoctrinator, 2014

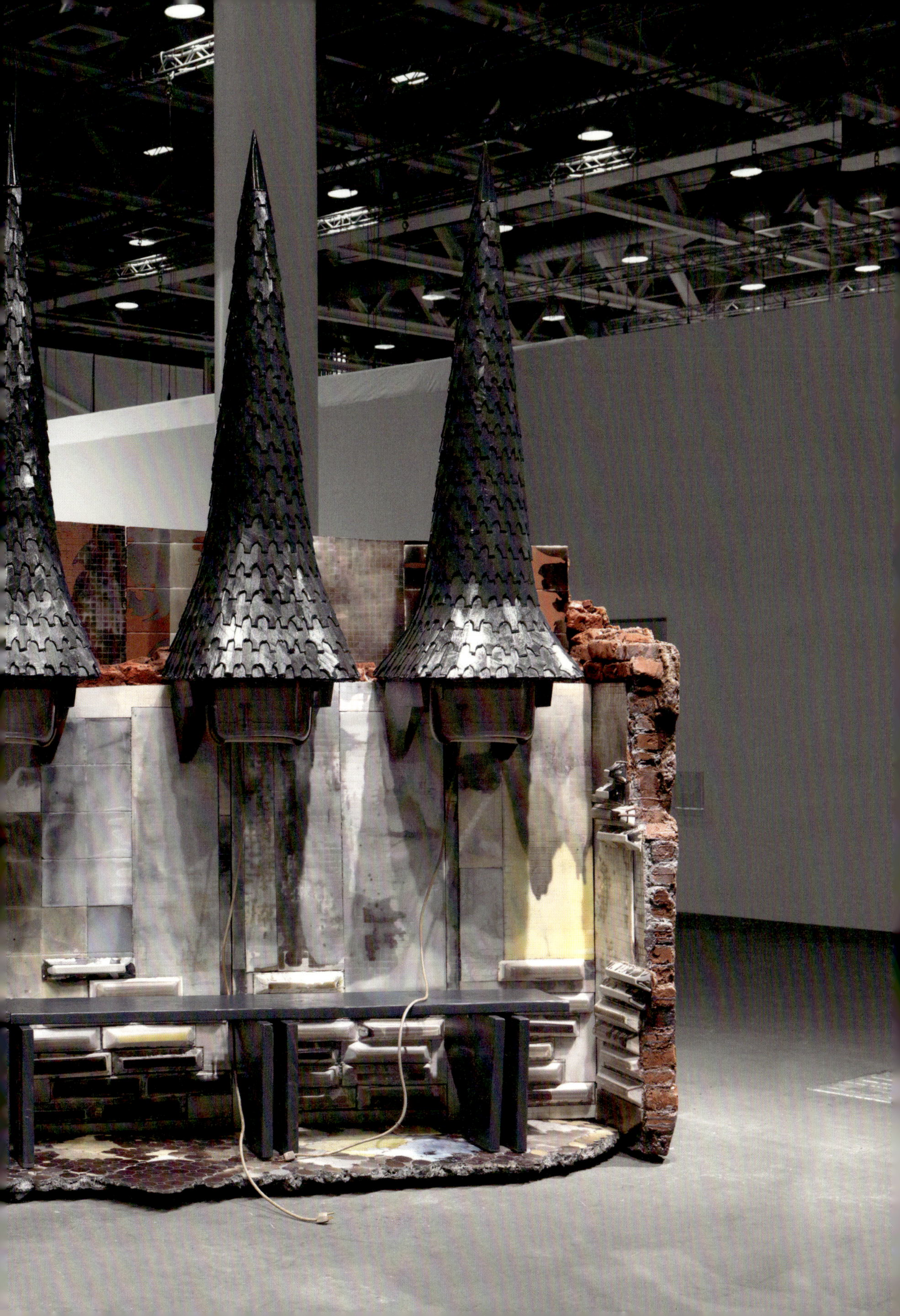

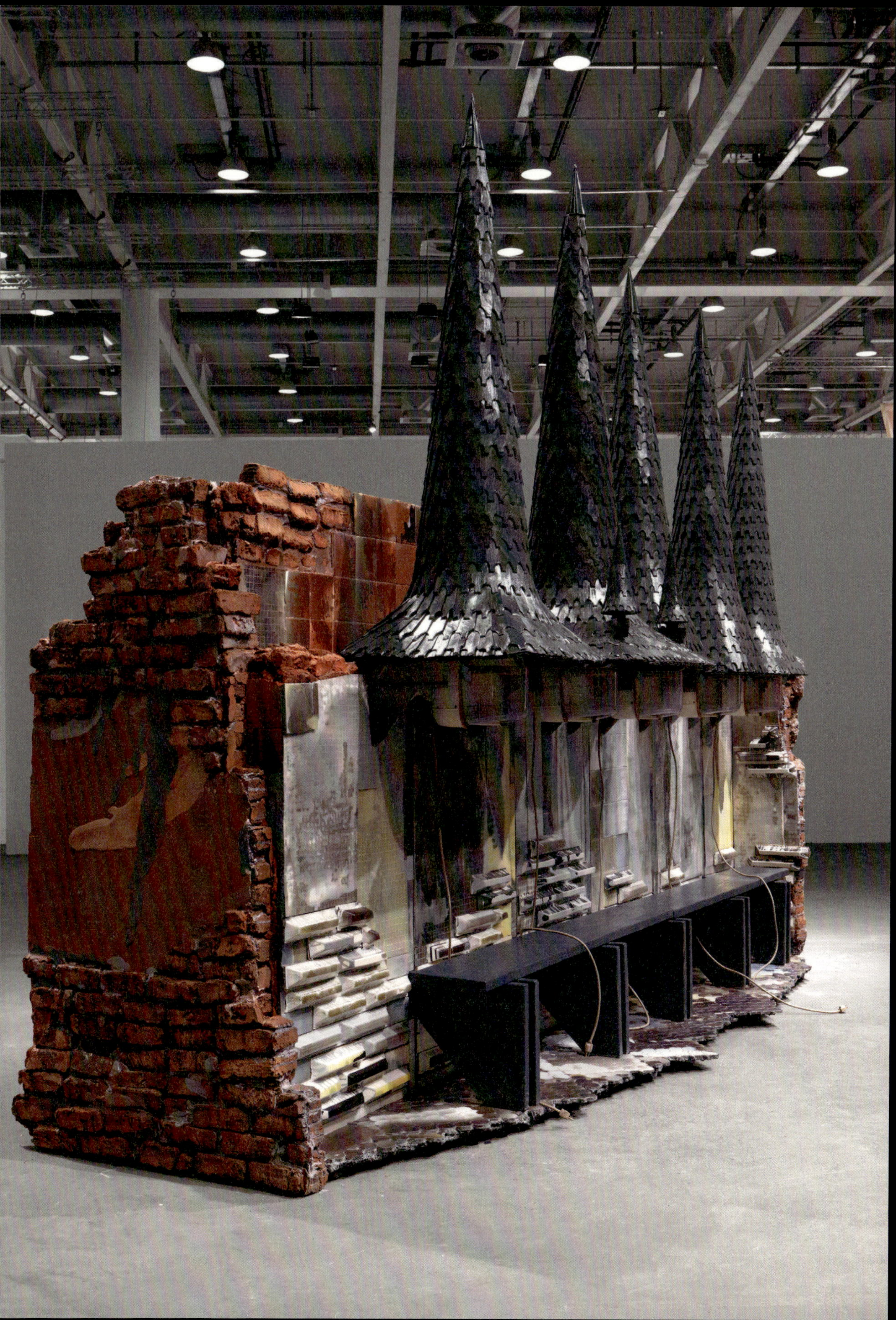

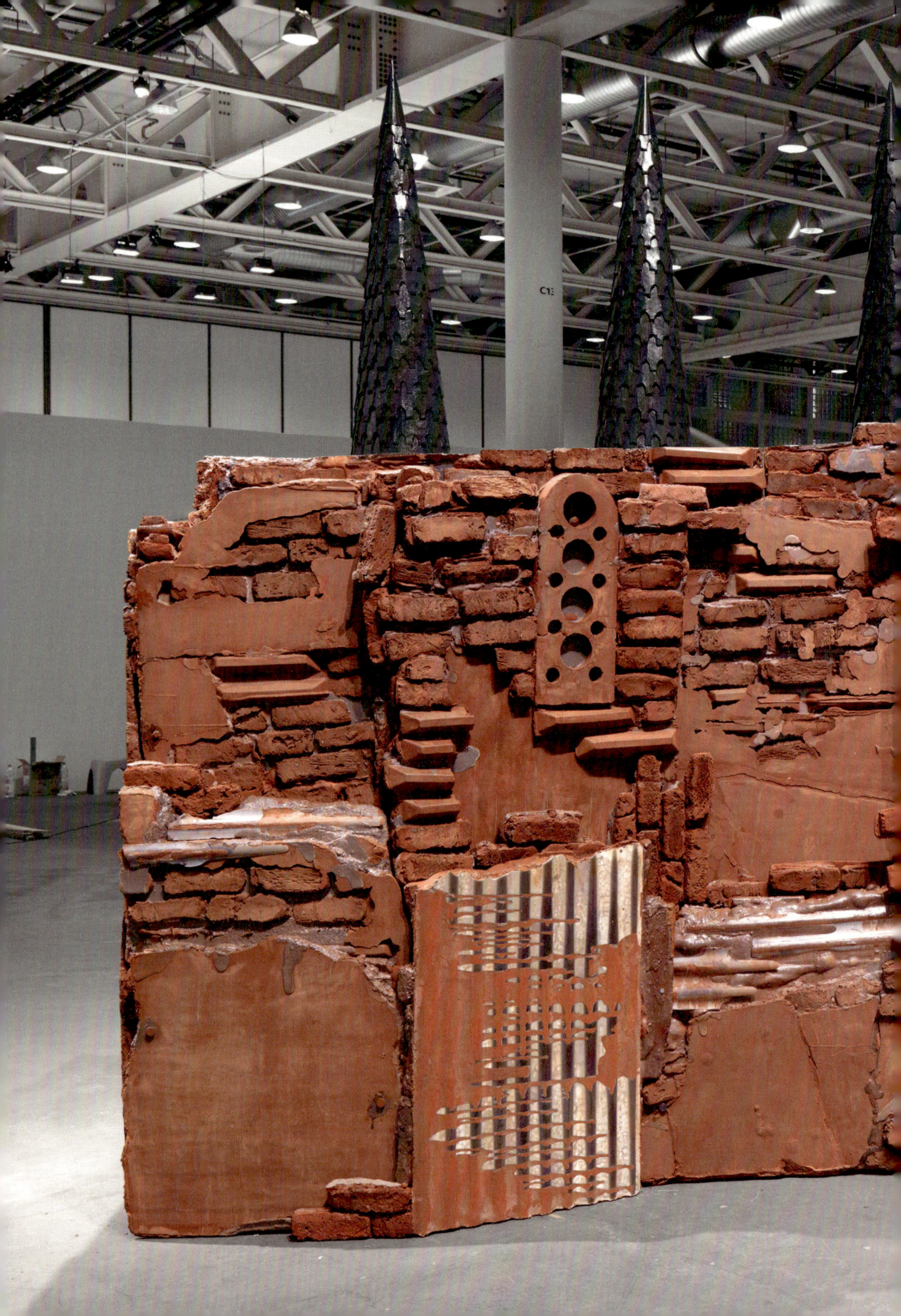
C13

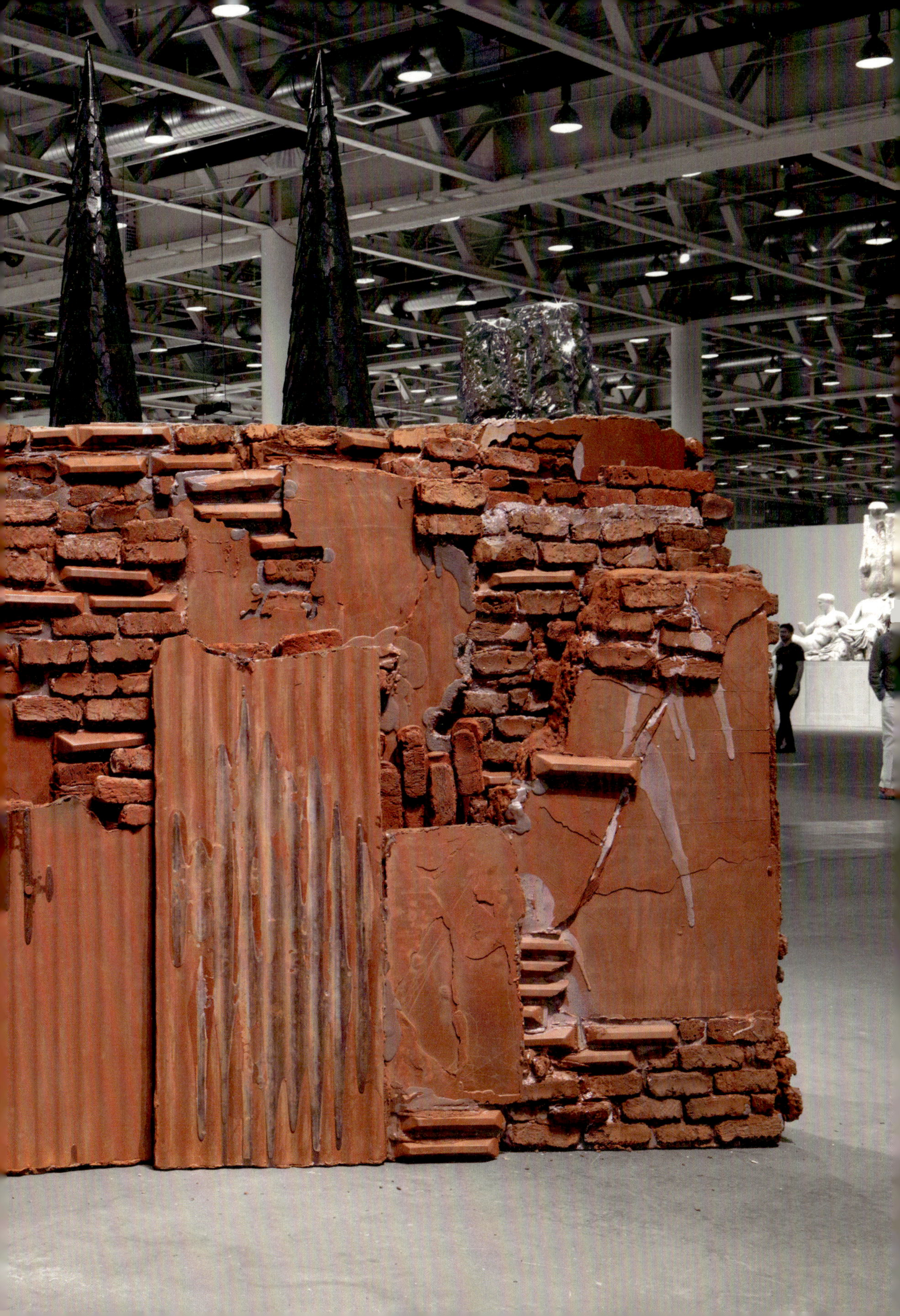

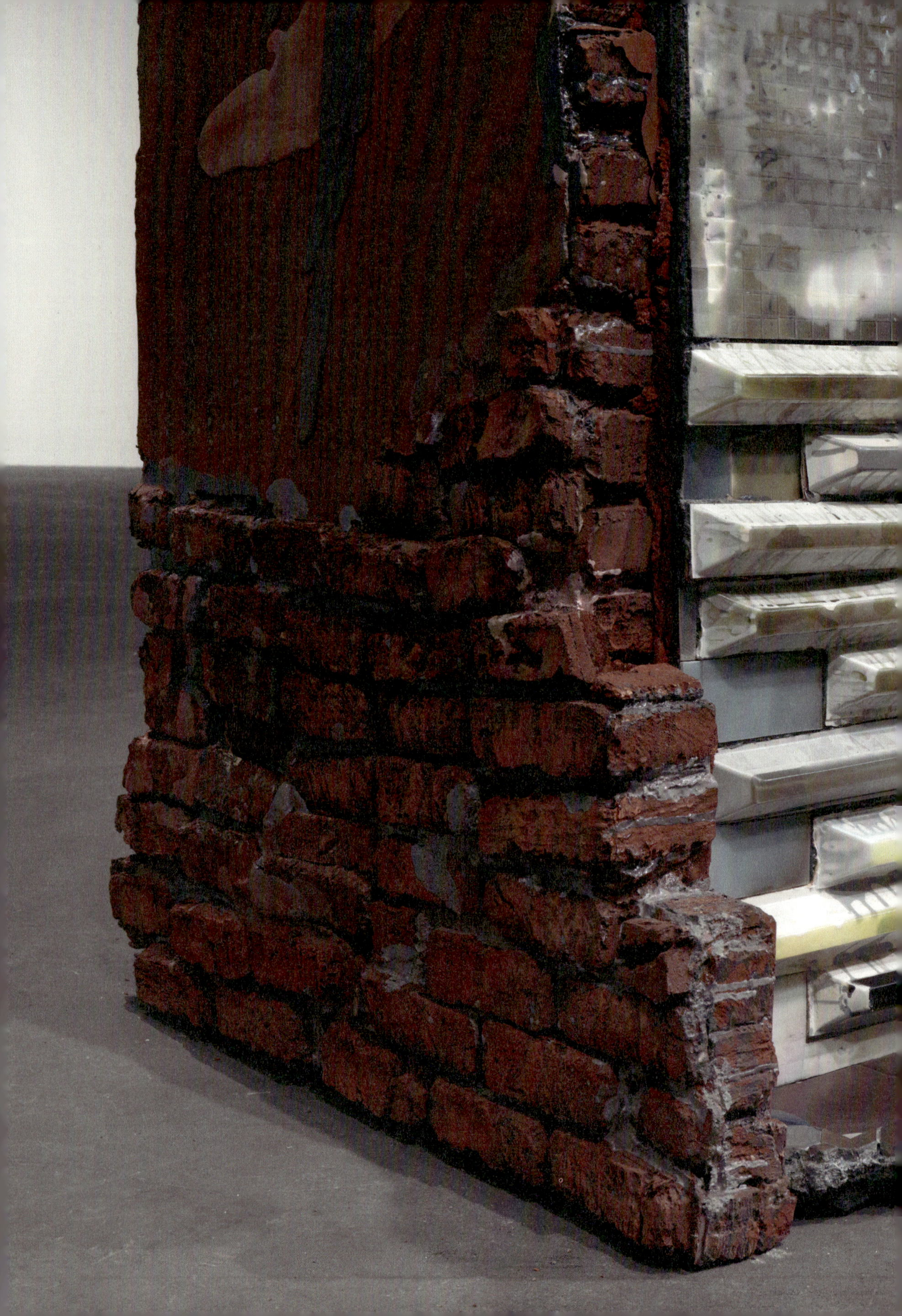

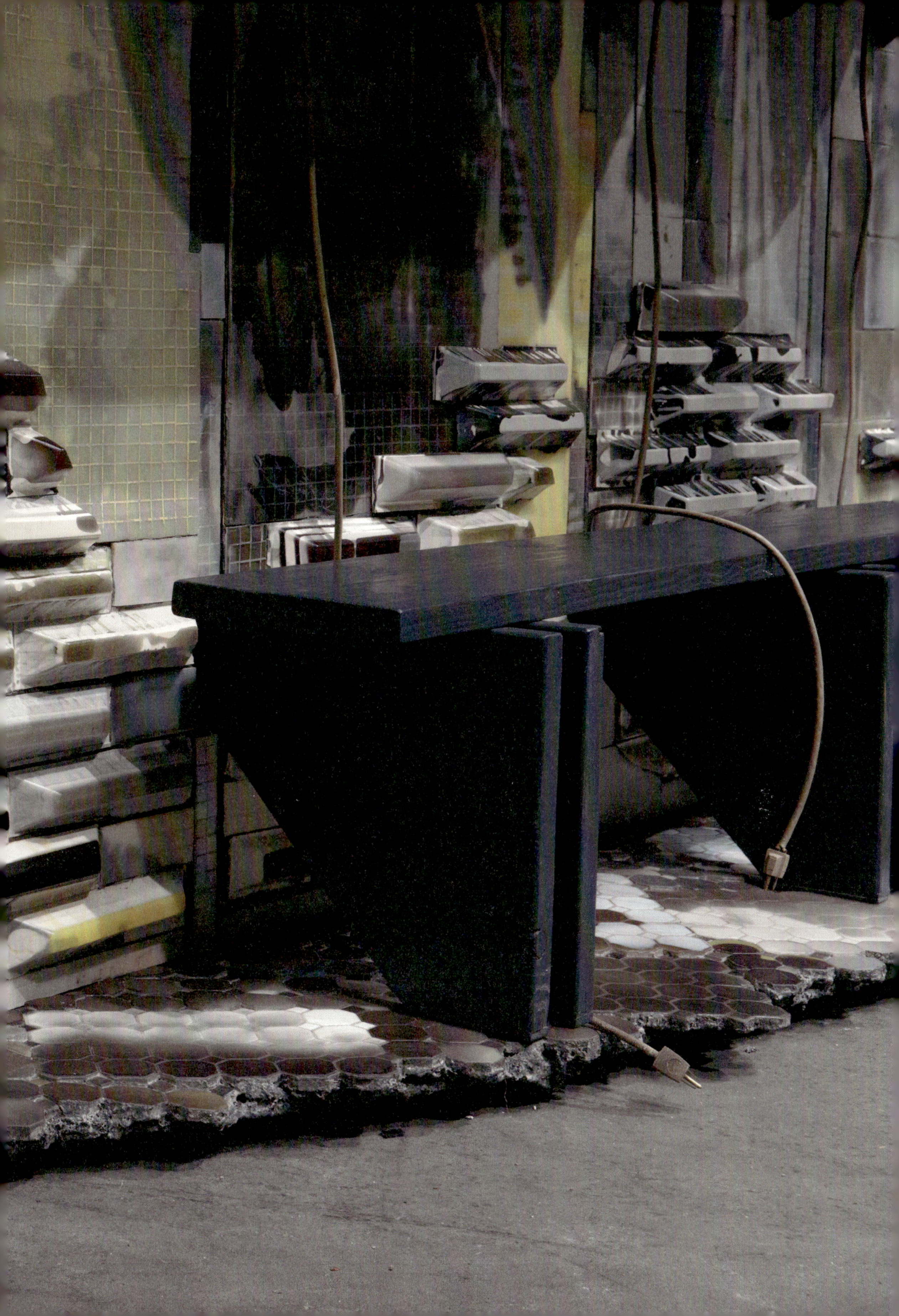

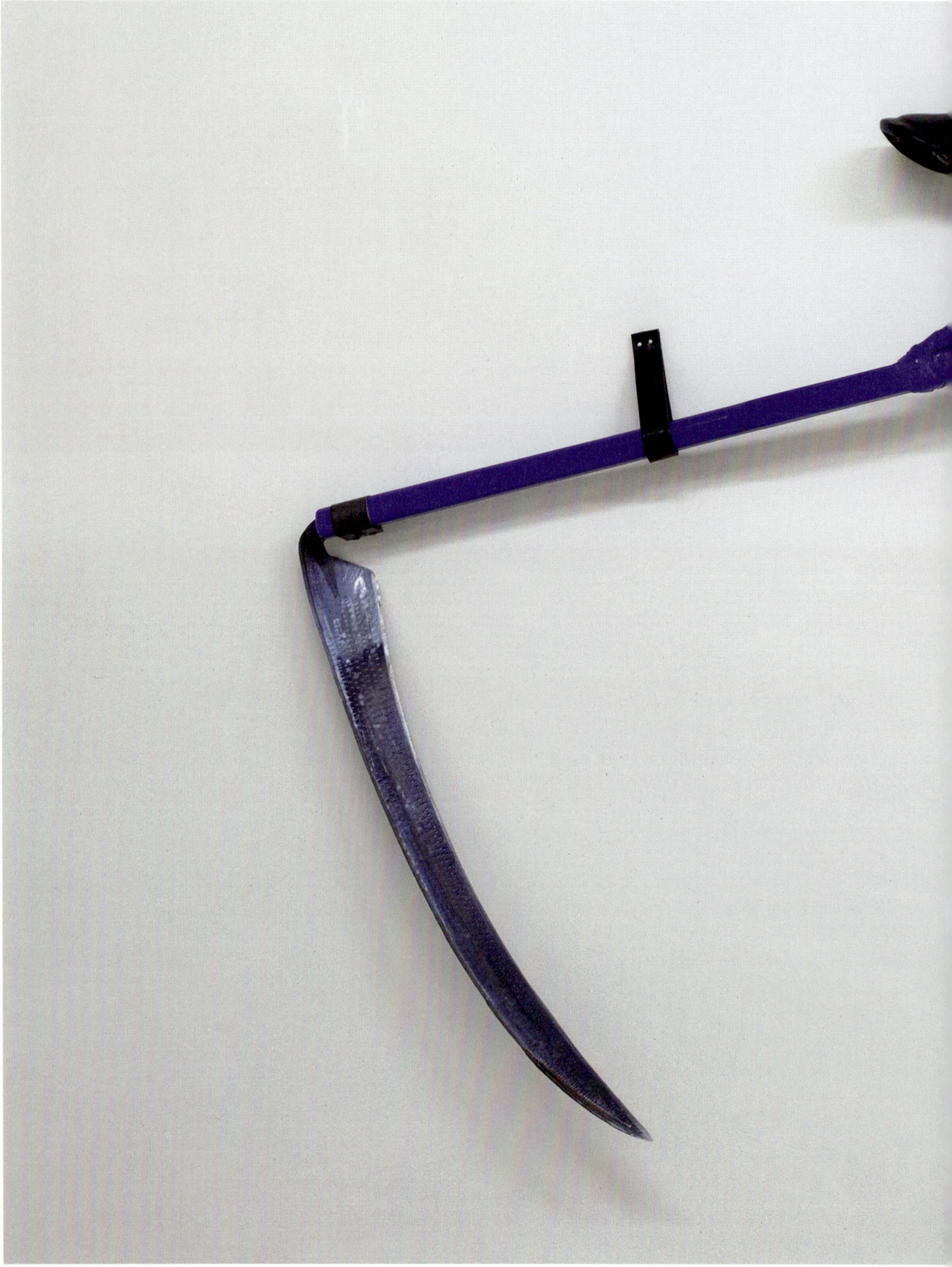

Untitled, 2014

CruciFritz, 2014

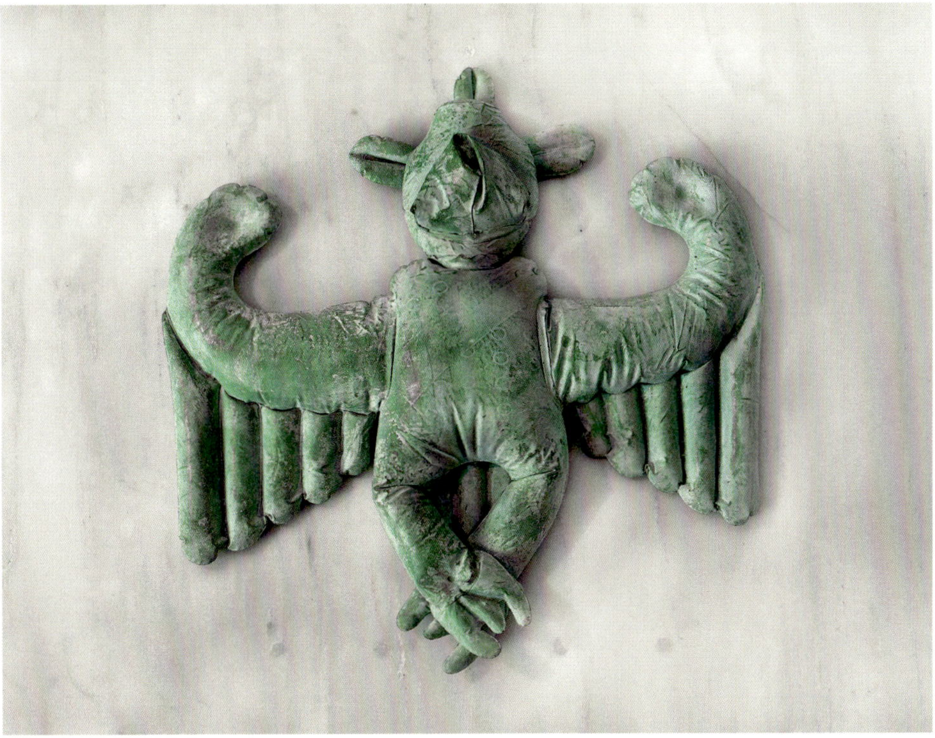

Conversion Table, 2014

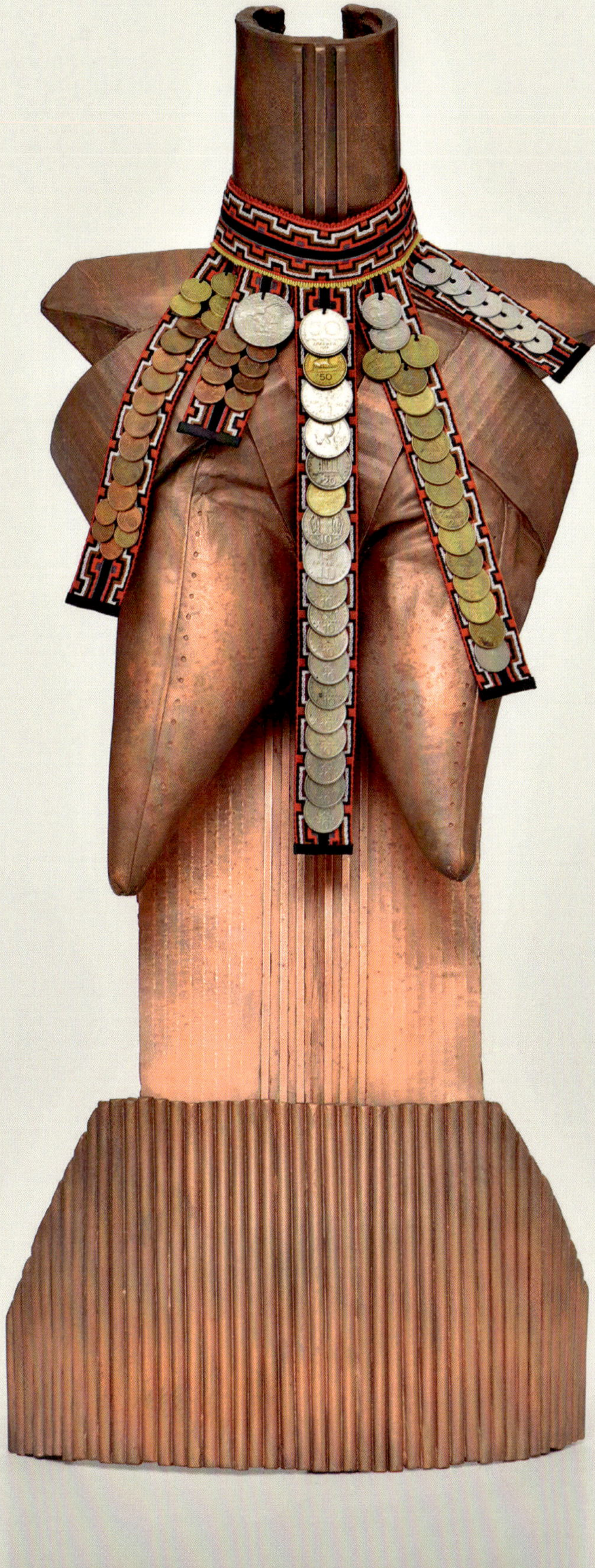

Atrophy Room, 2015

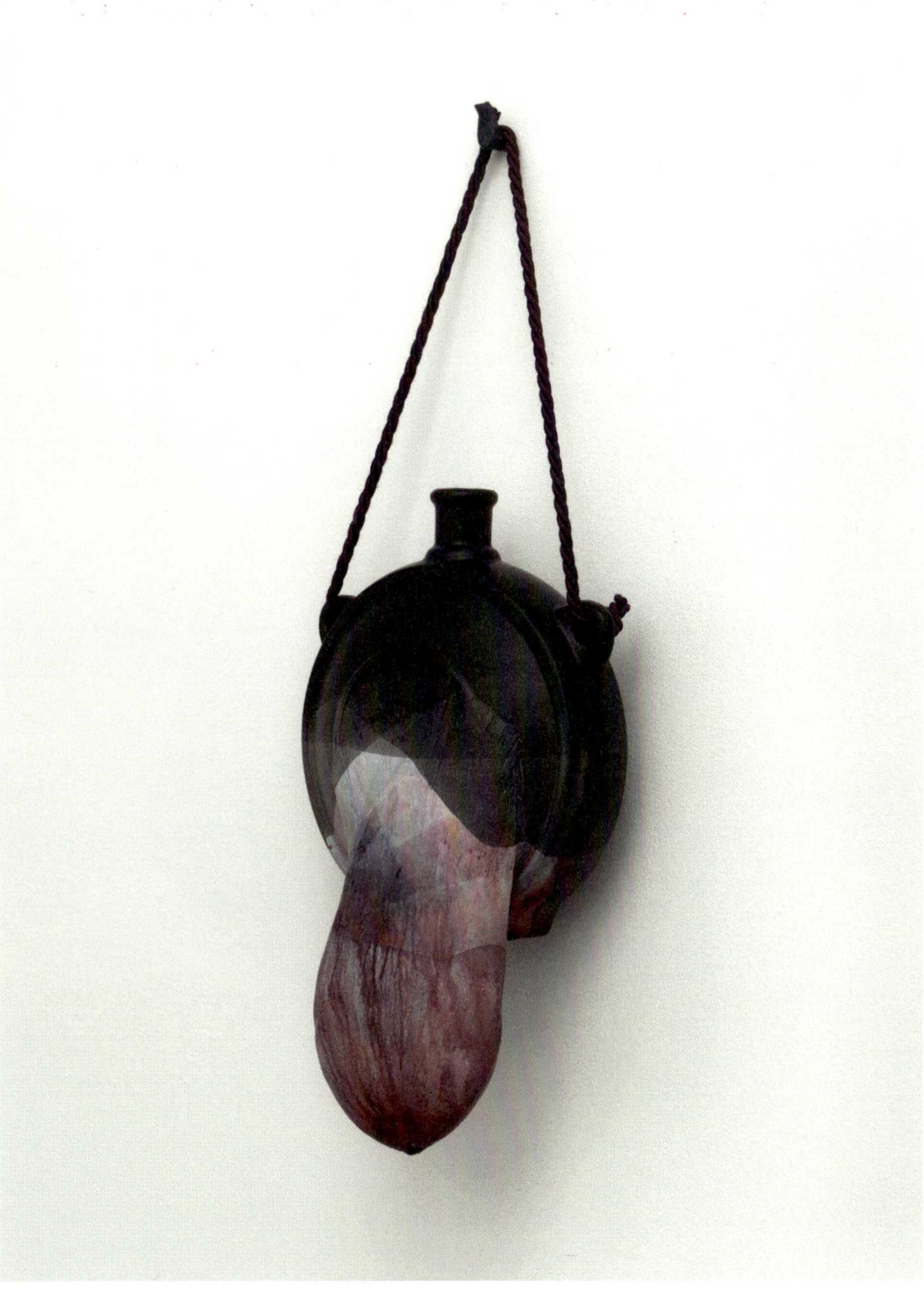

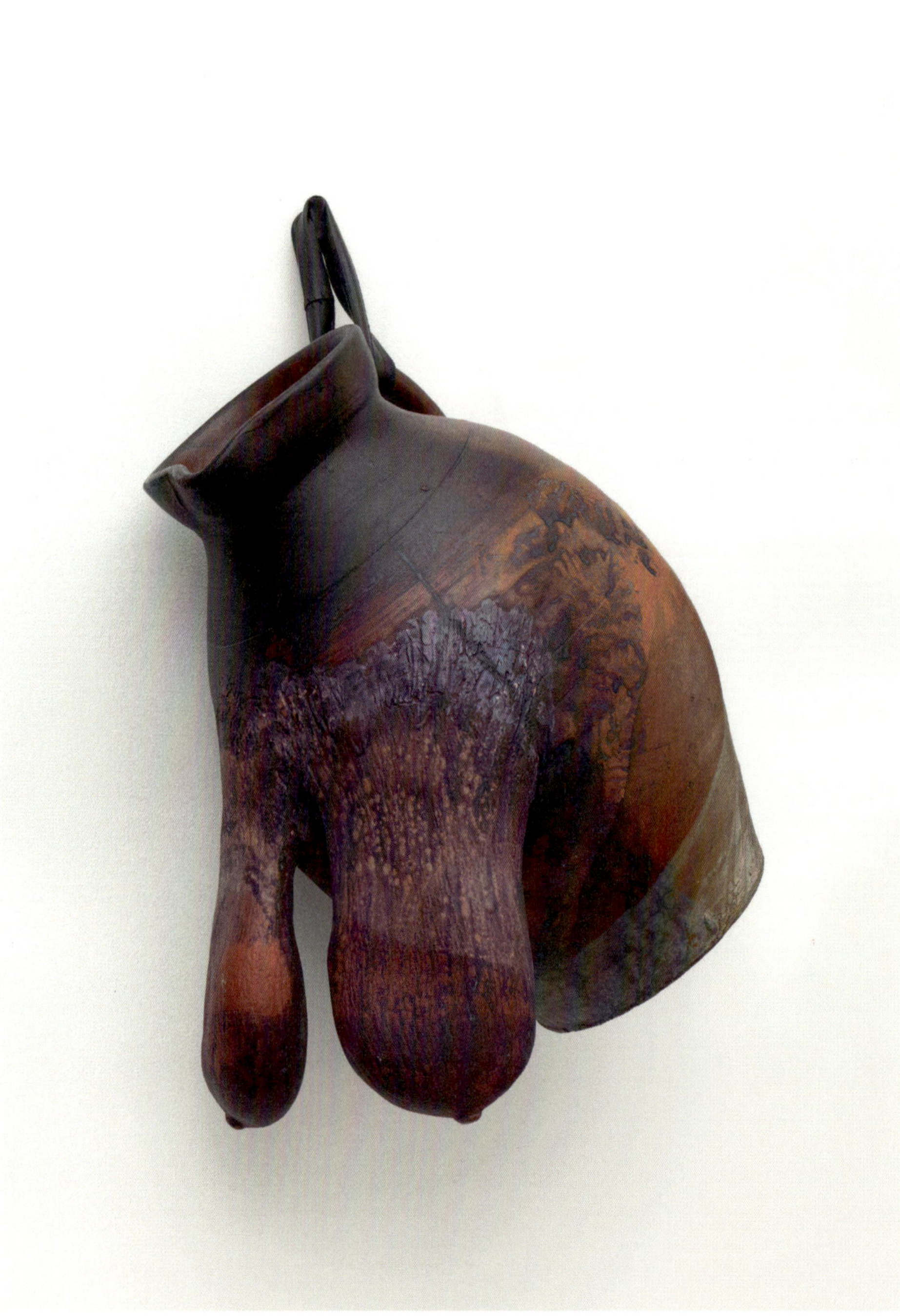

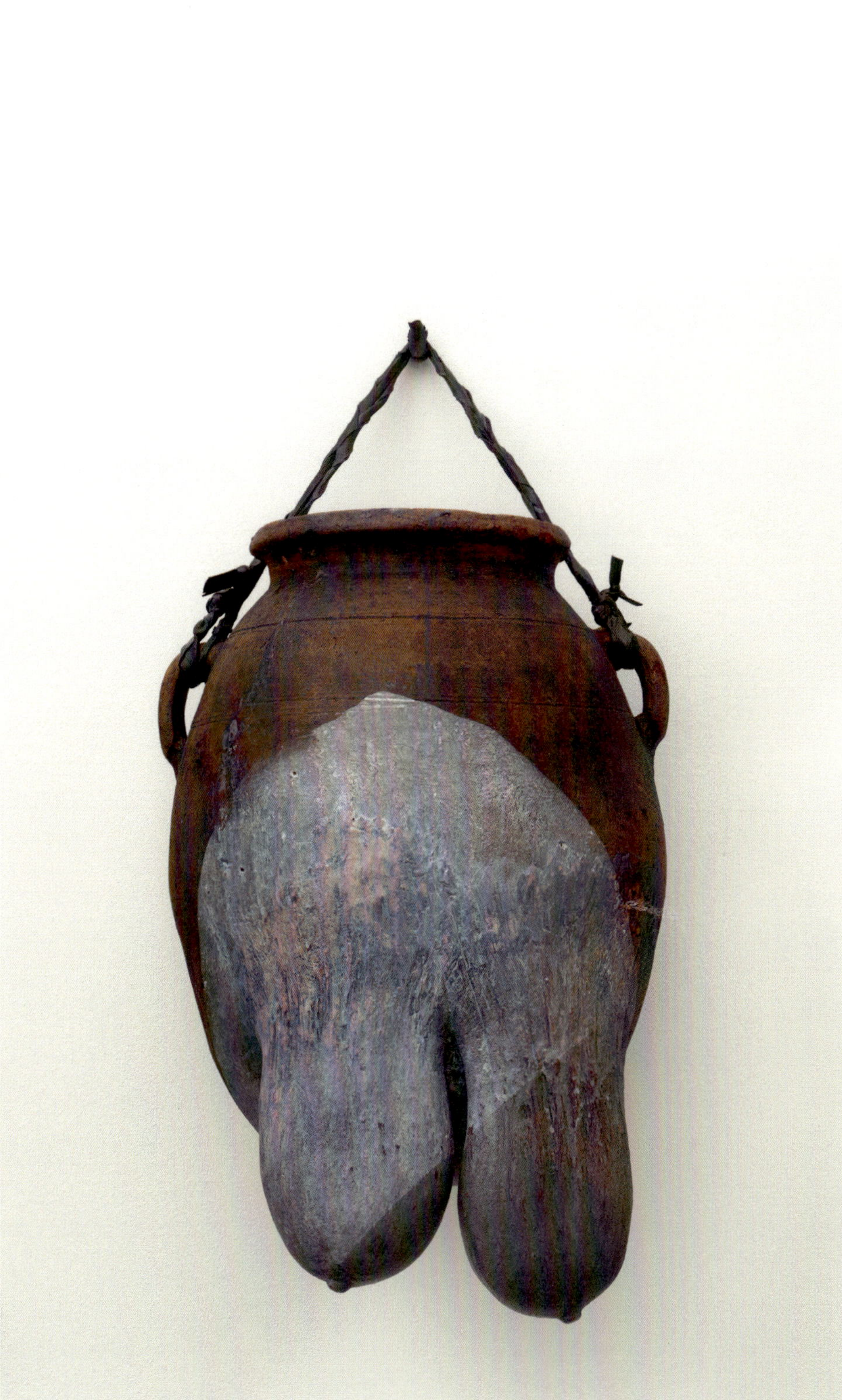

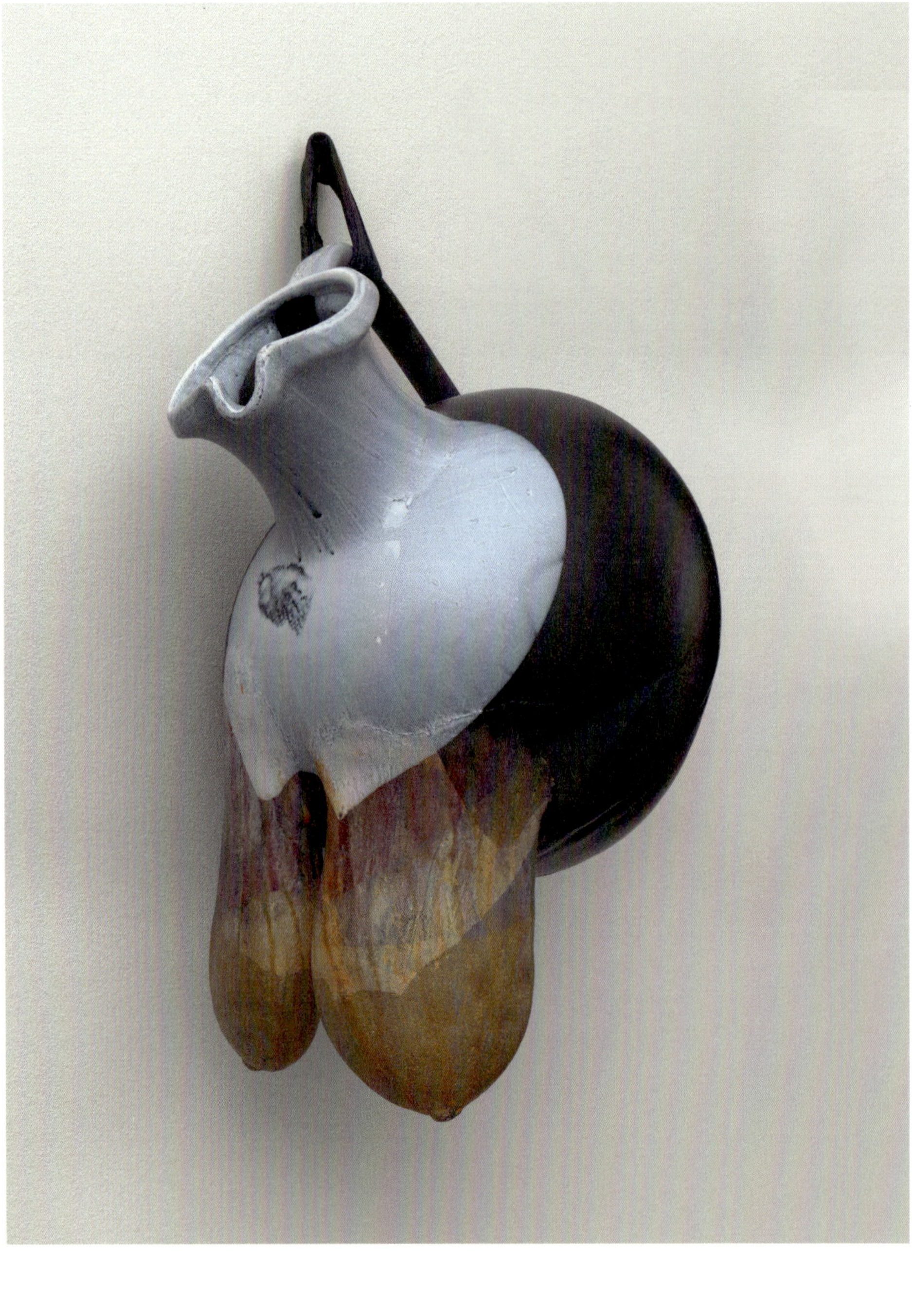

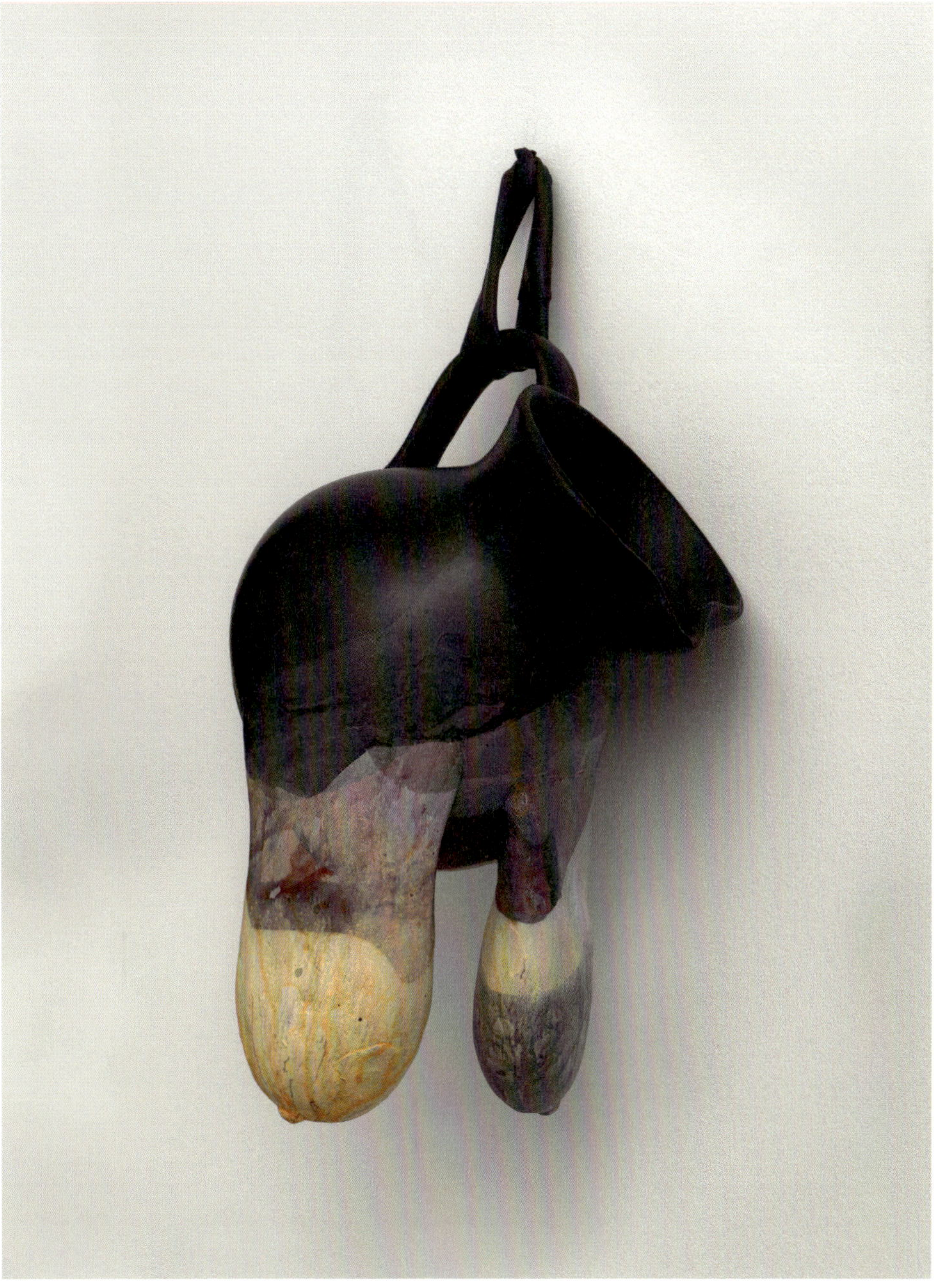

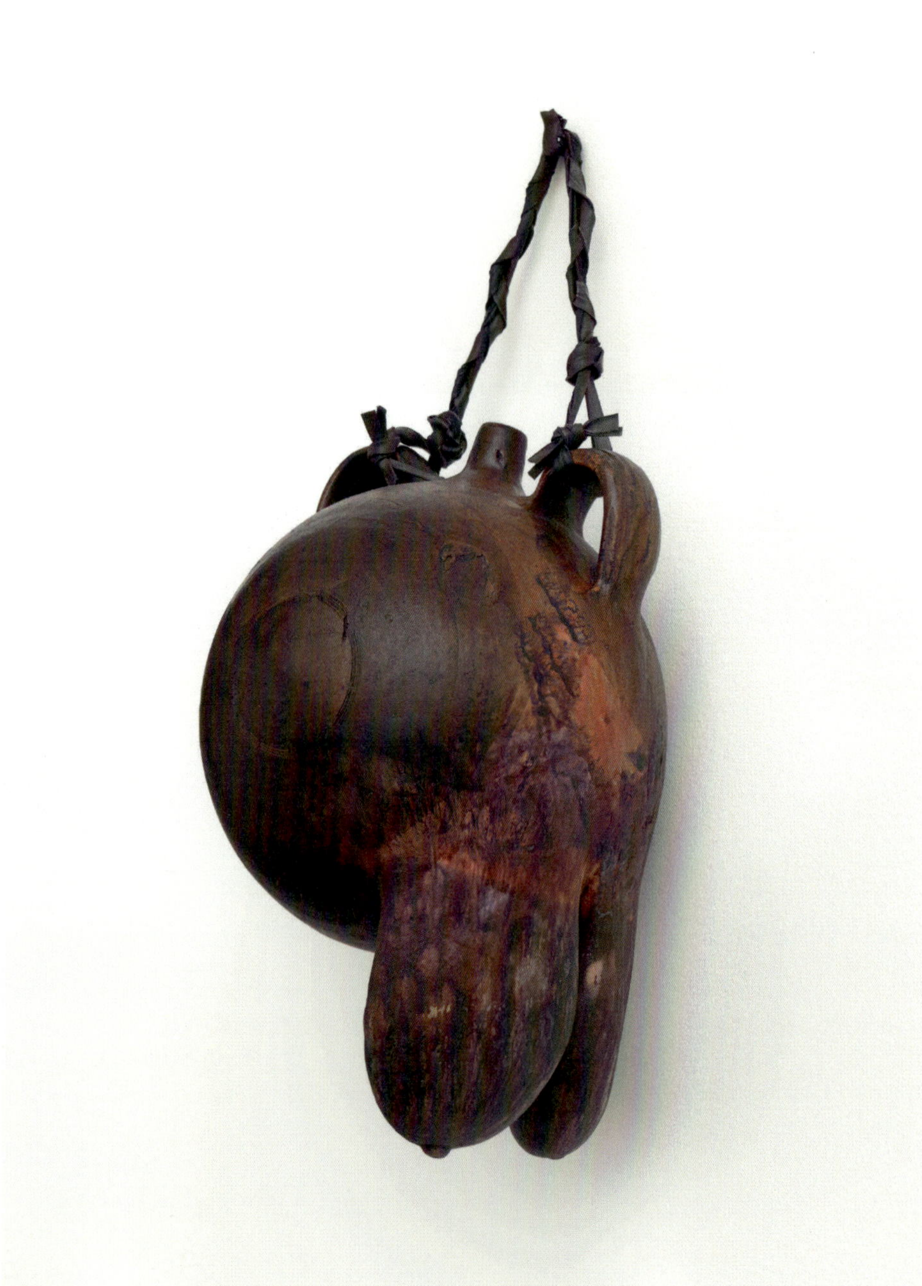

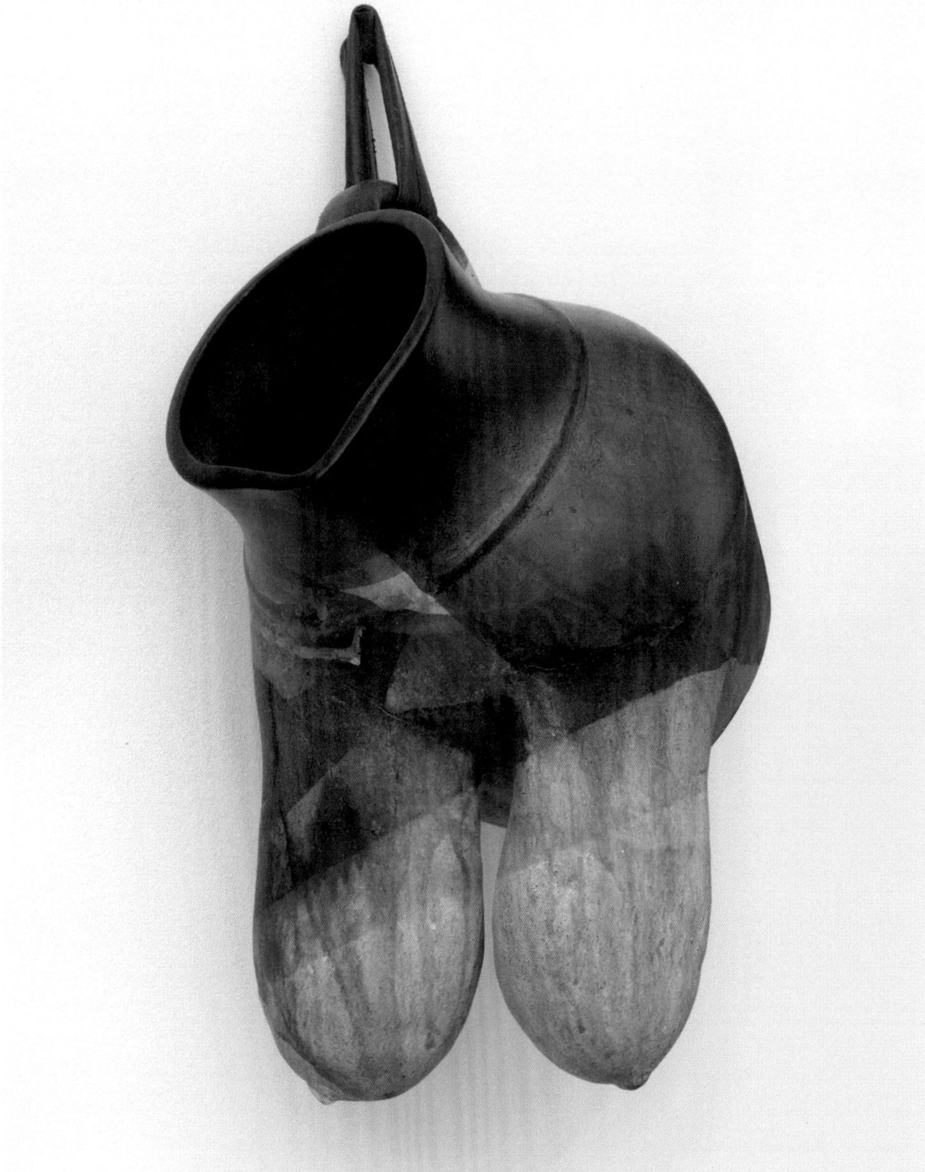

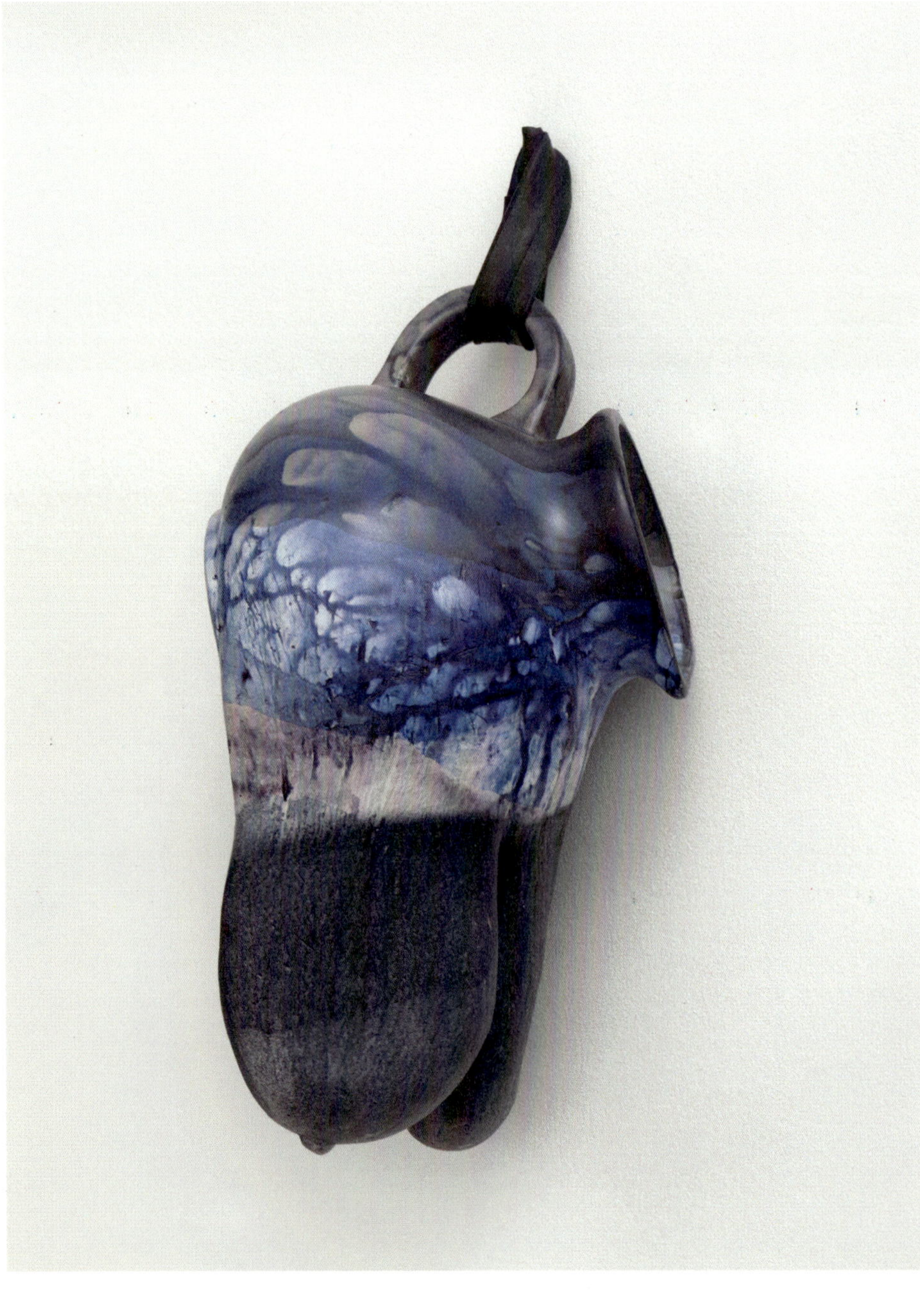

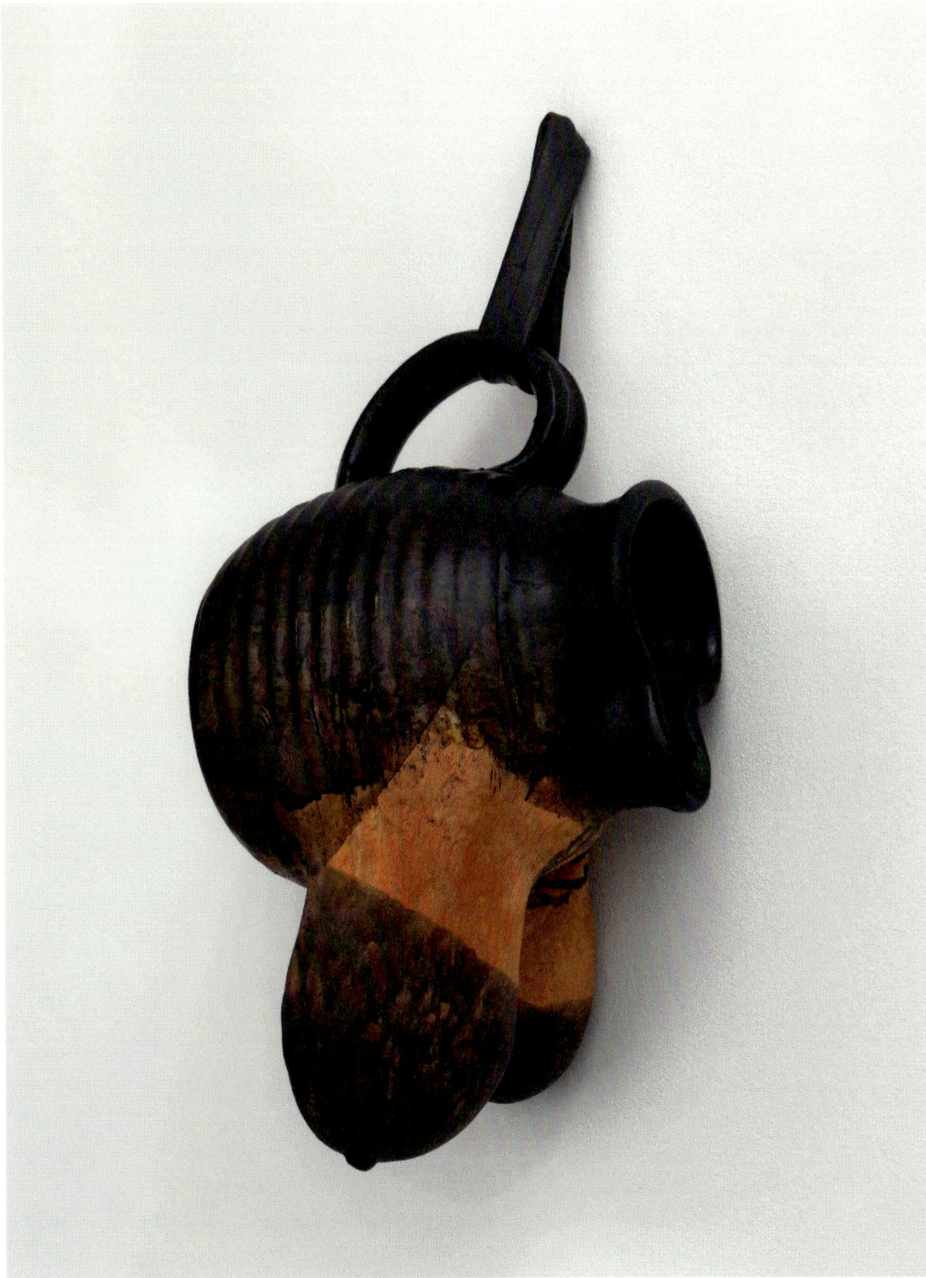

Guarda Che Luna, 2015

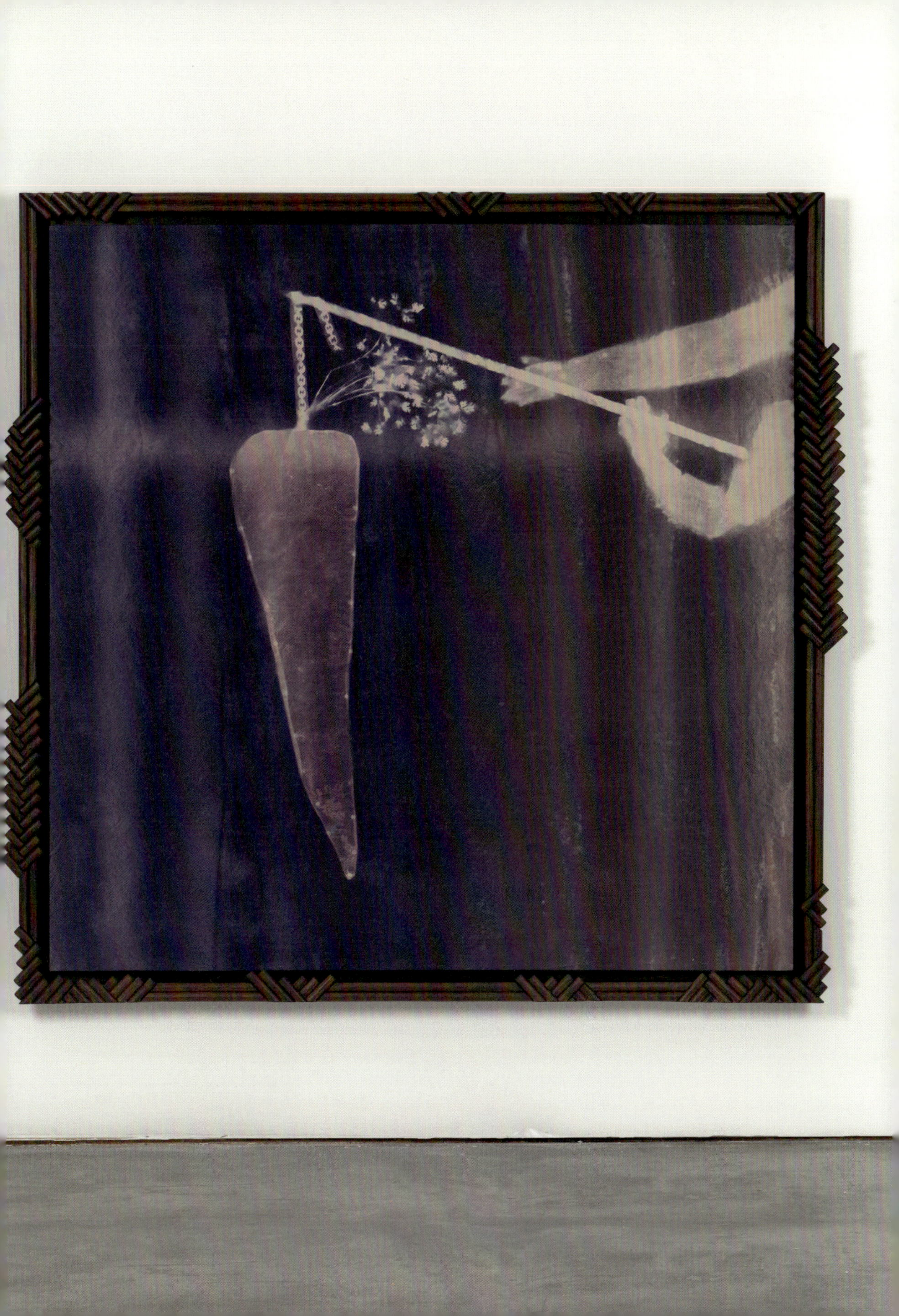

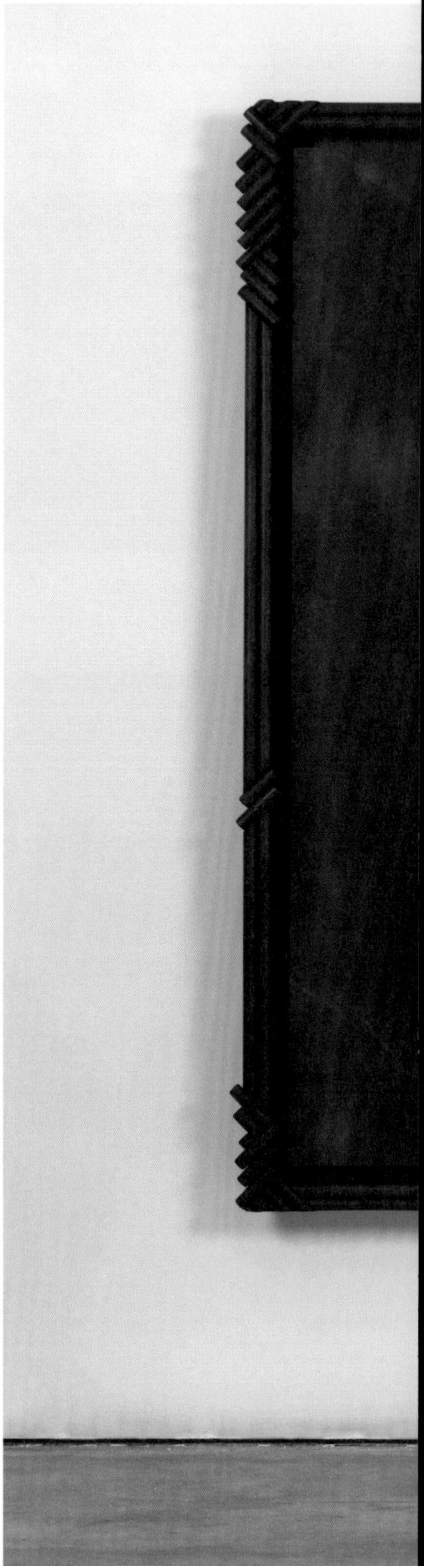

Slavesitting, 2015

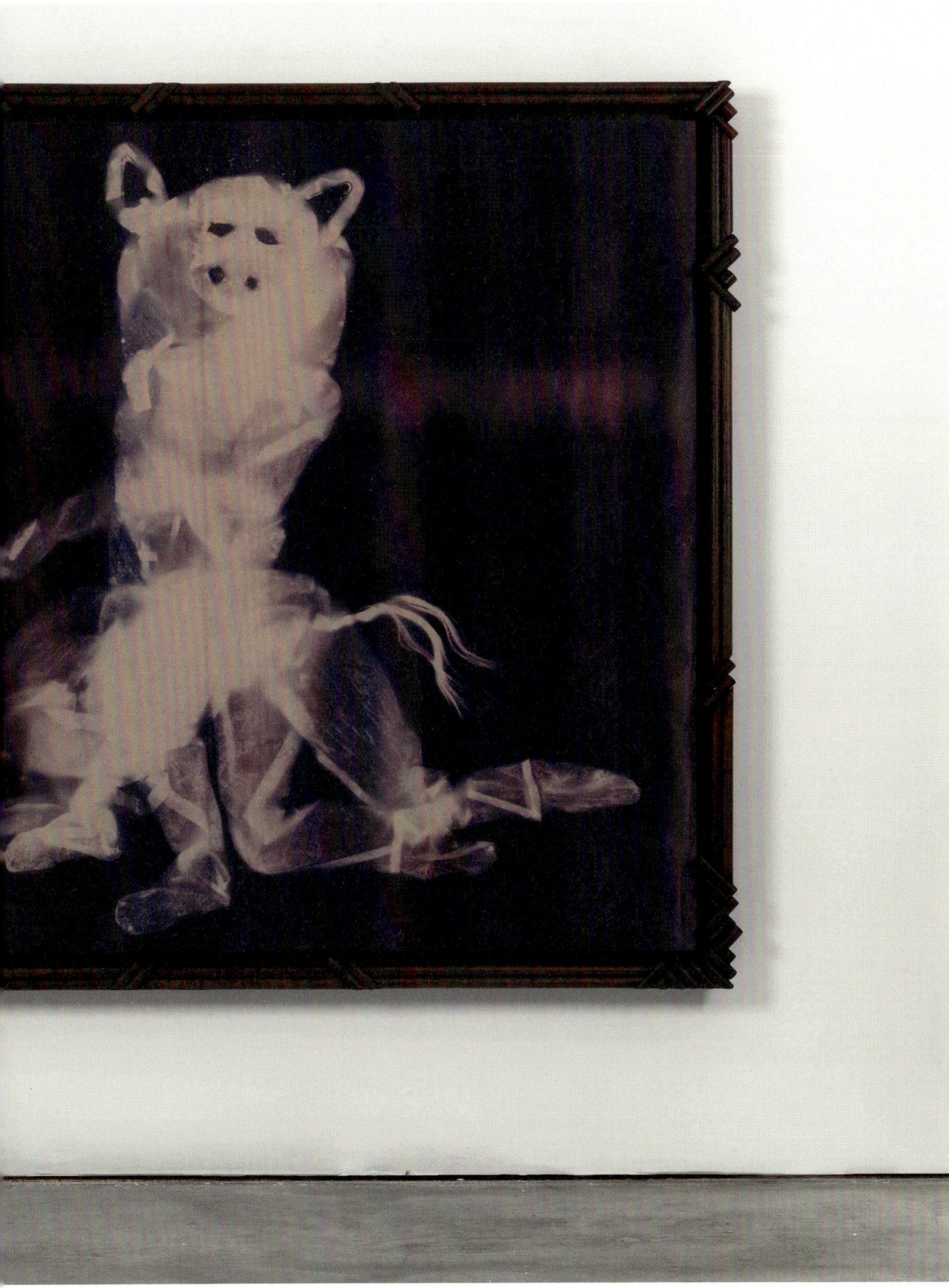

Summer Kampf, 2015

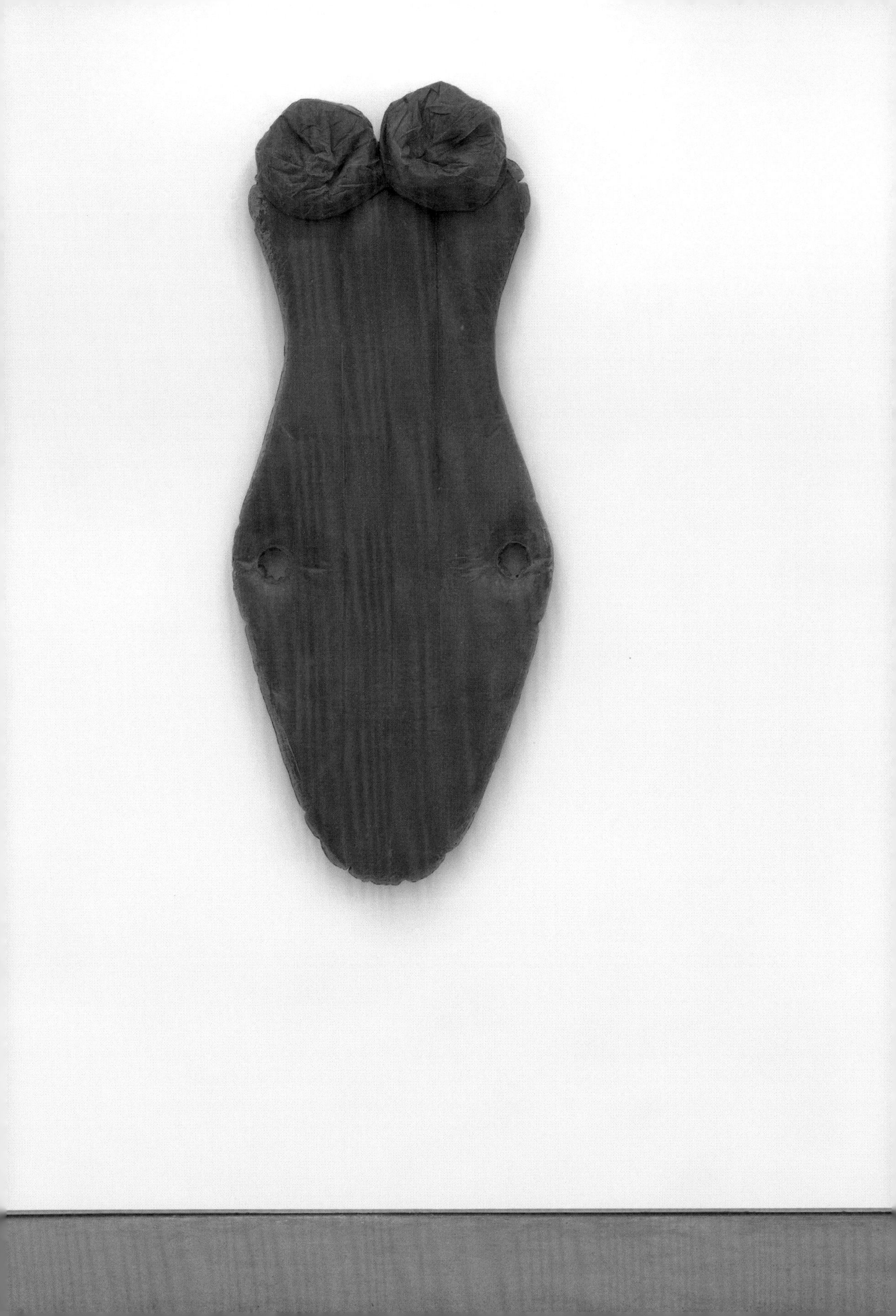

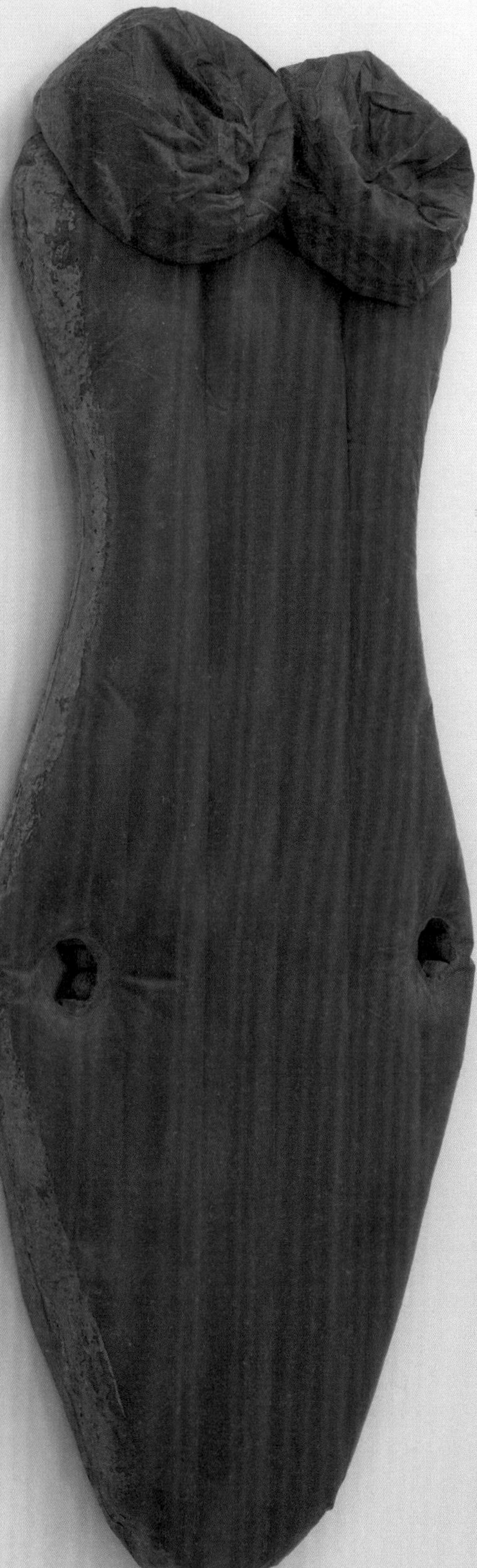

Tomatopig, 2015

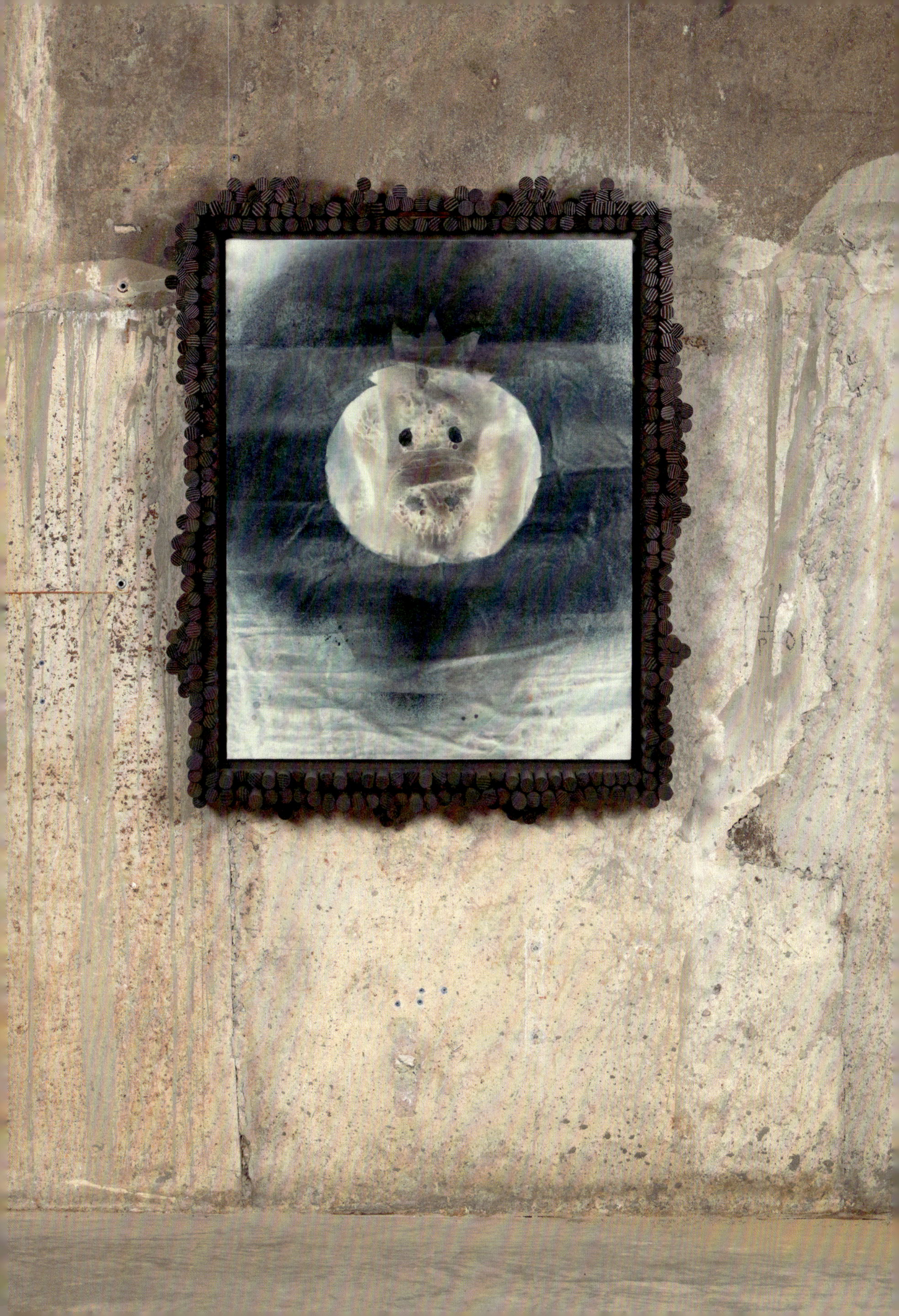

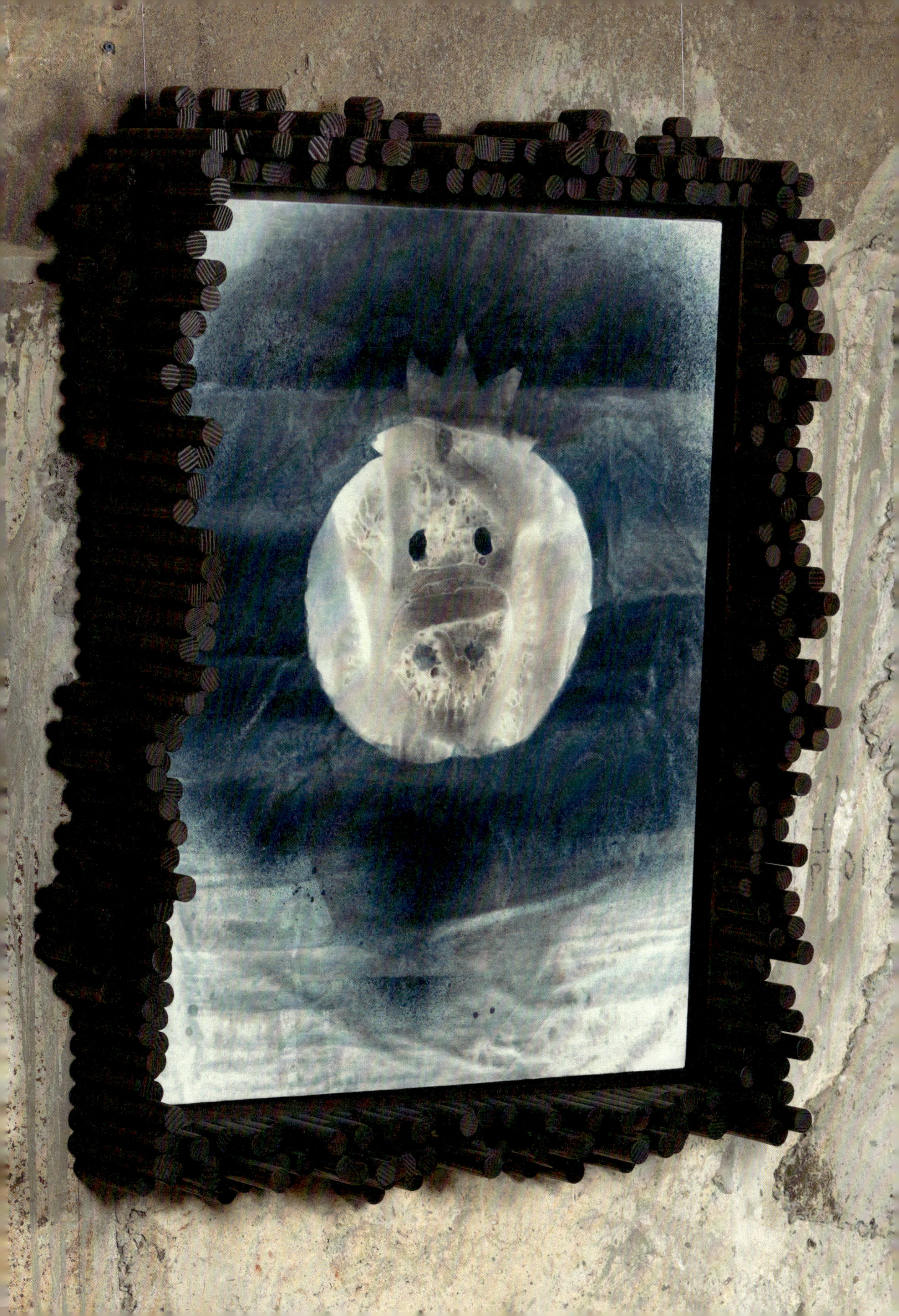

Untitled, 2015

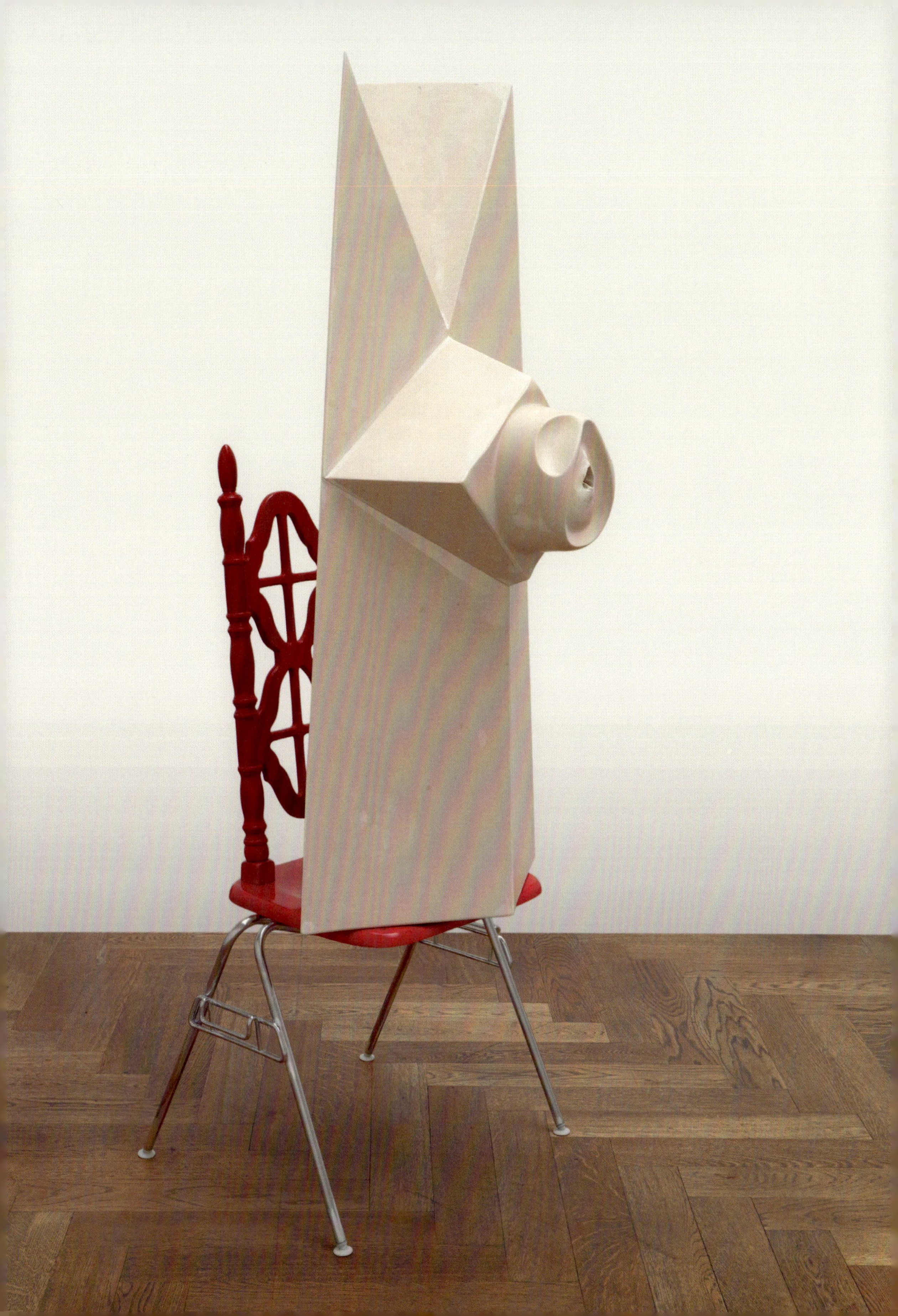

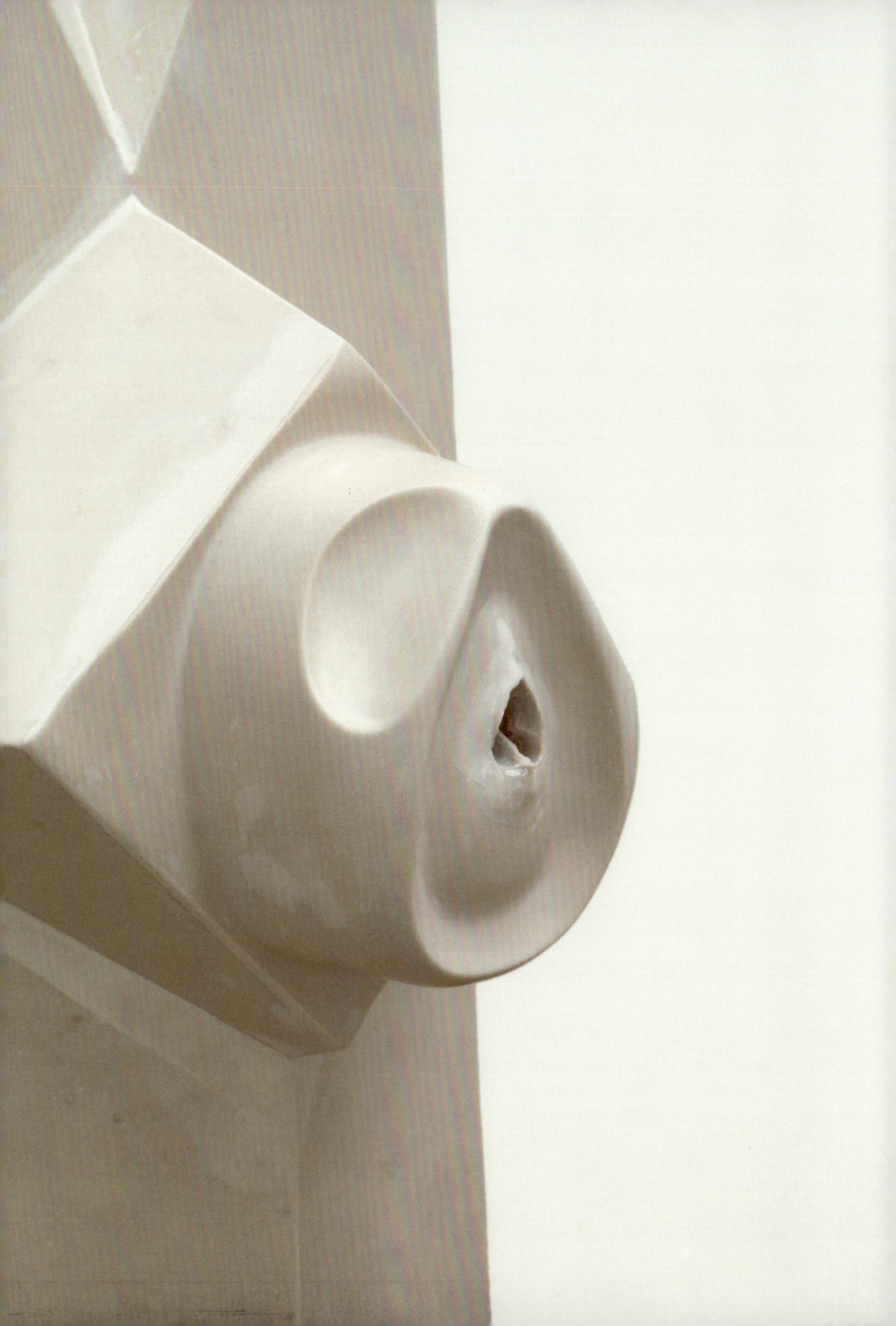

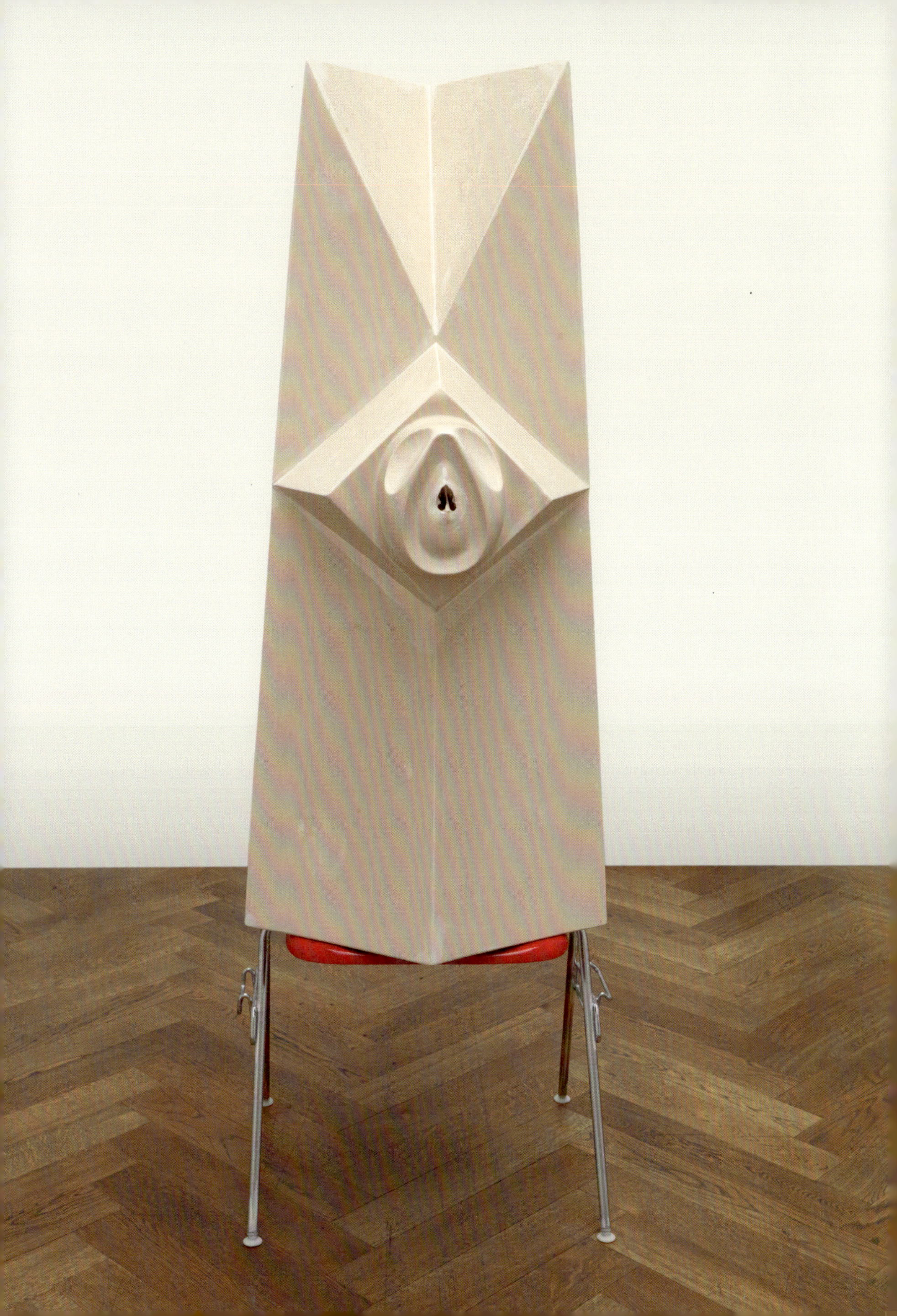

Untitled, 2015

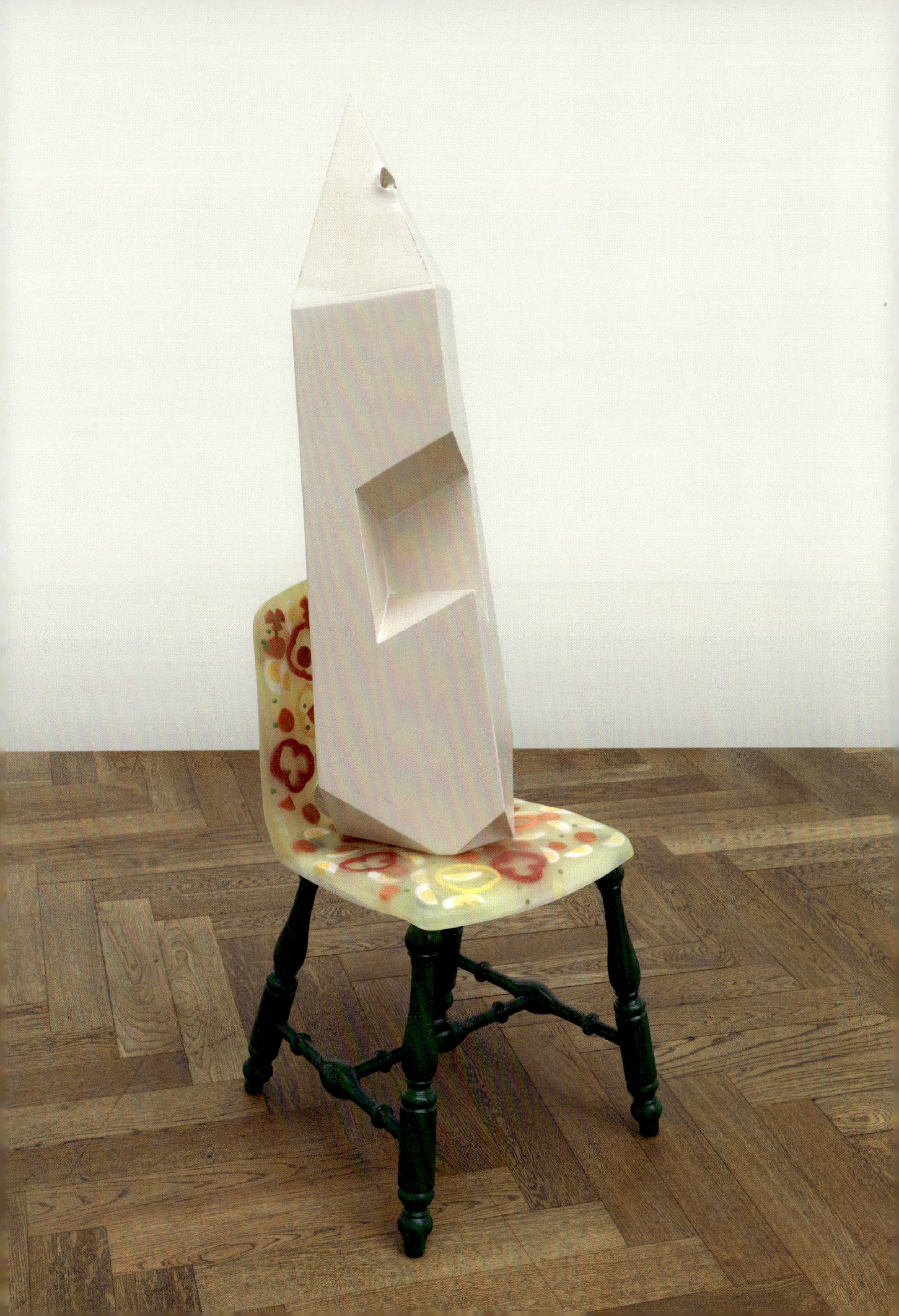

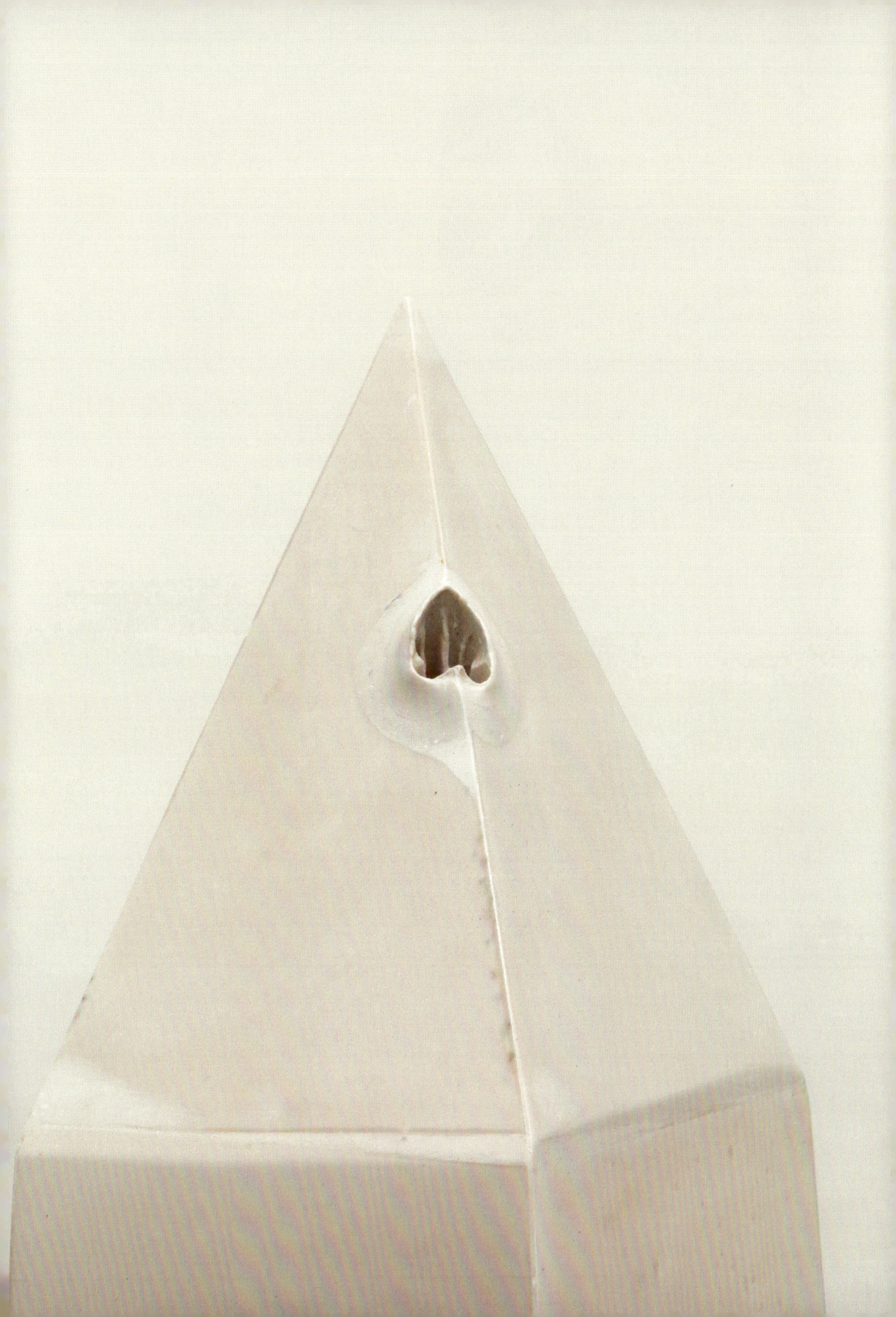

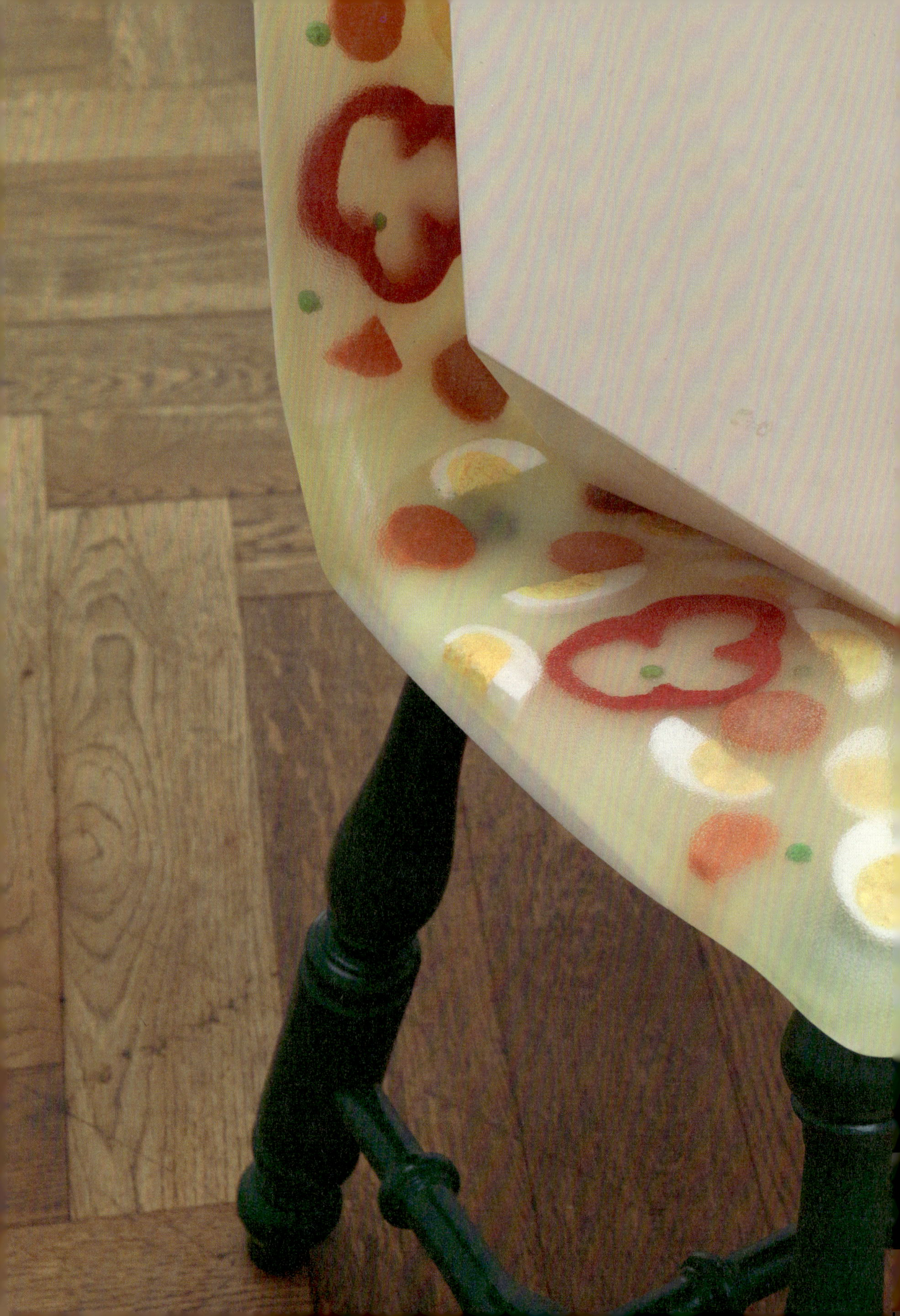

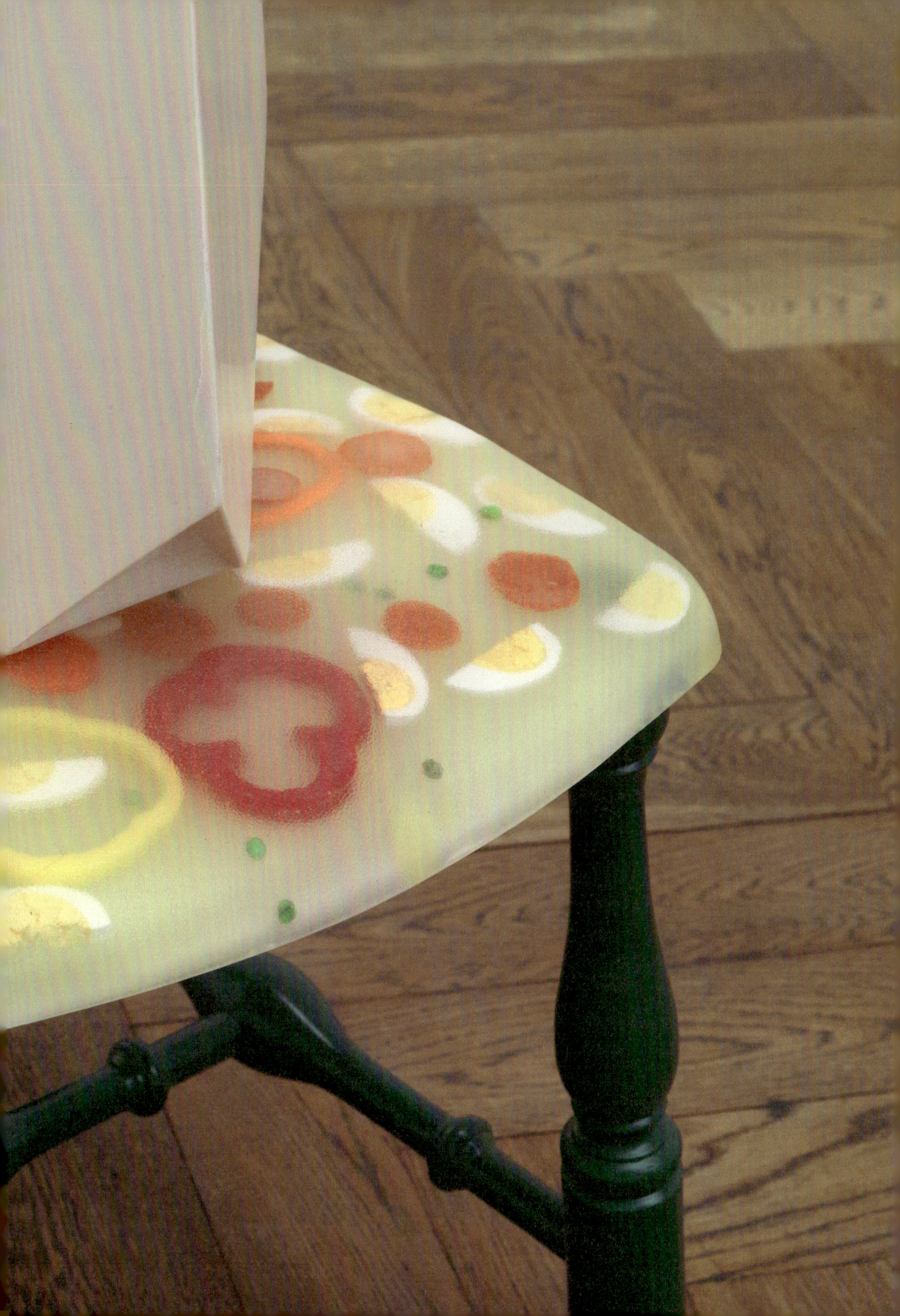

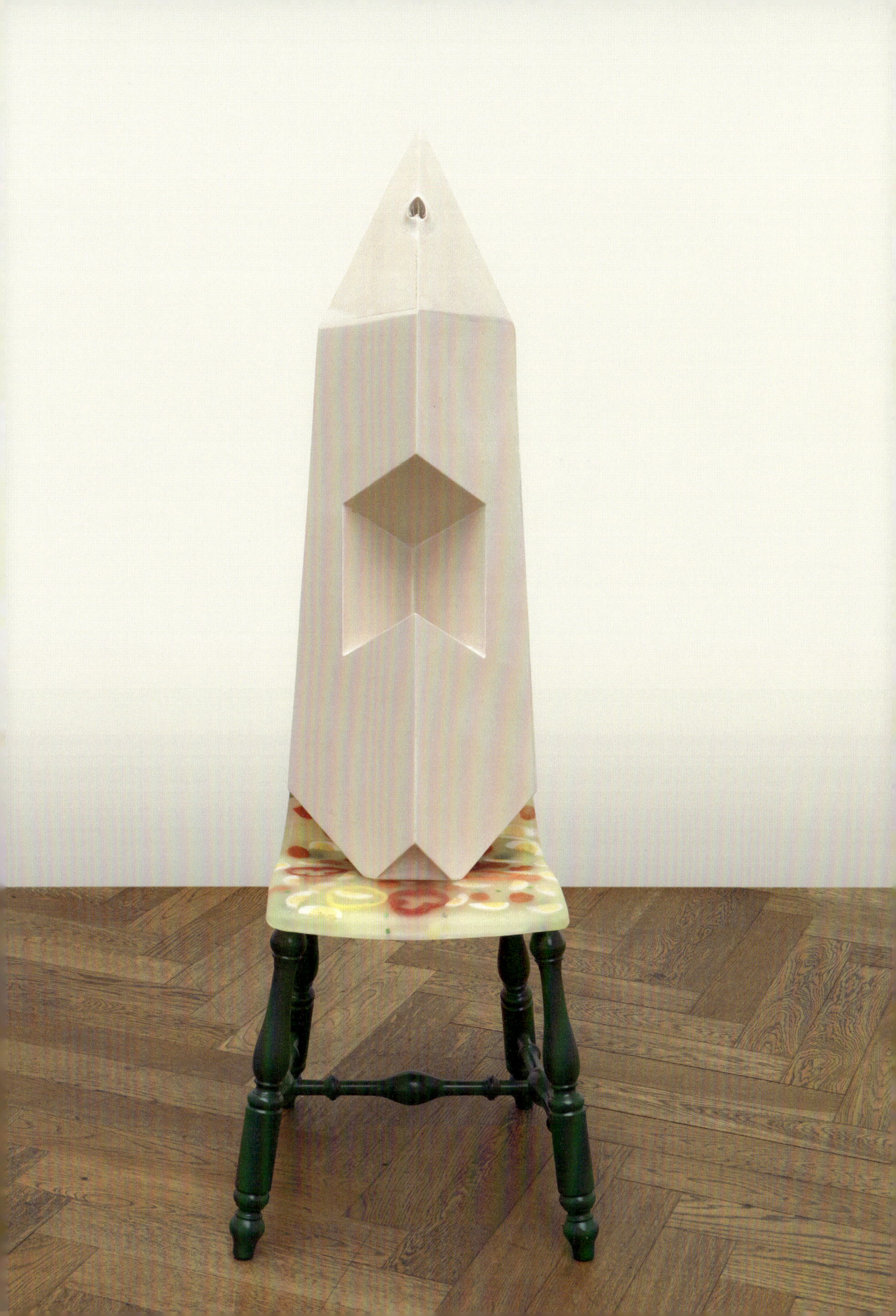

Commerce Exterieur Mondial Sentimental, 2017

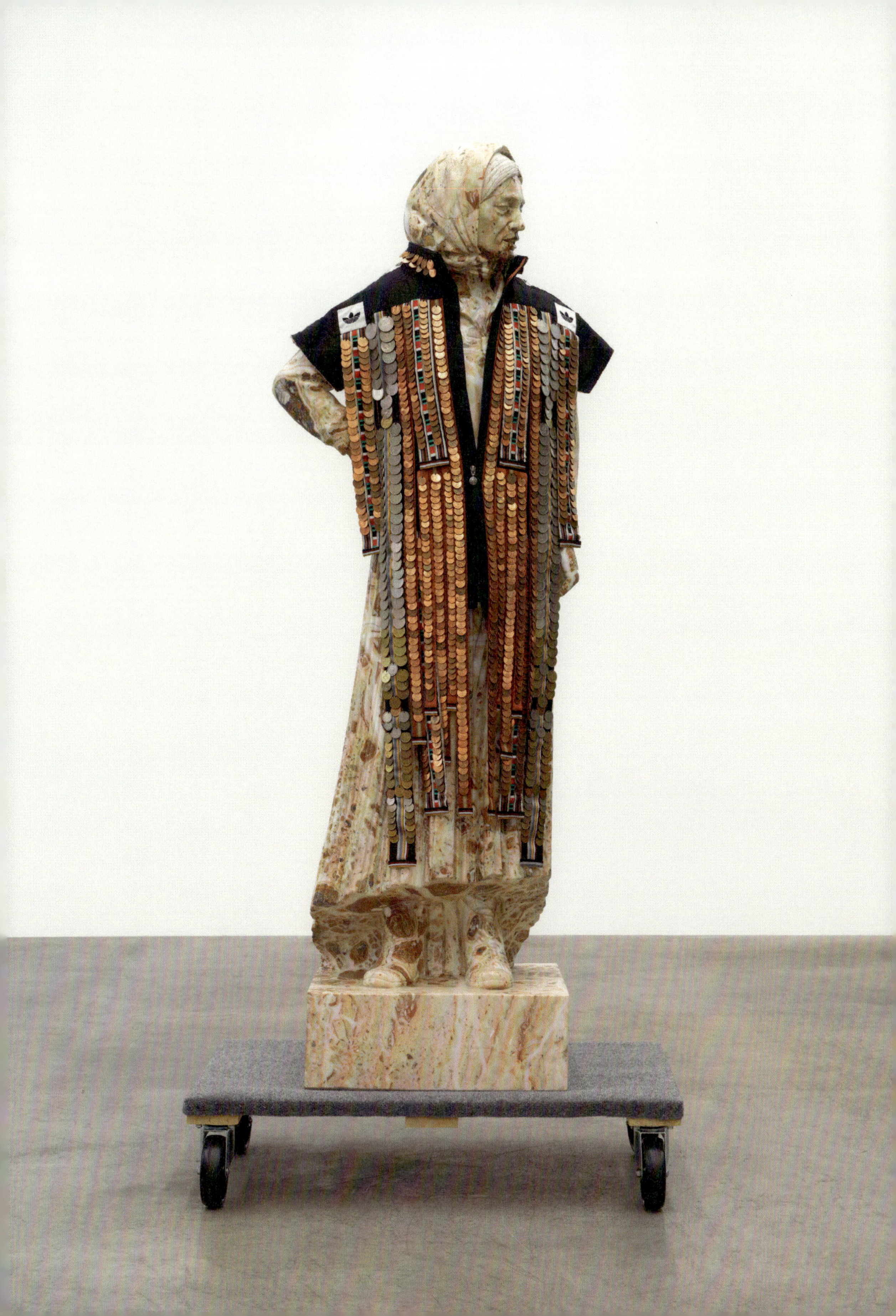

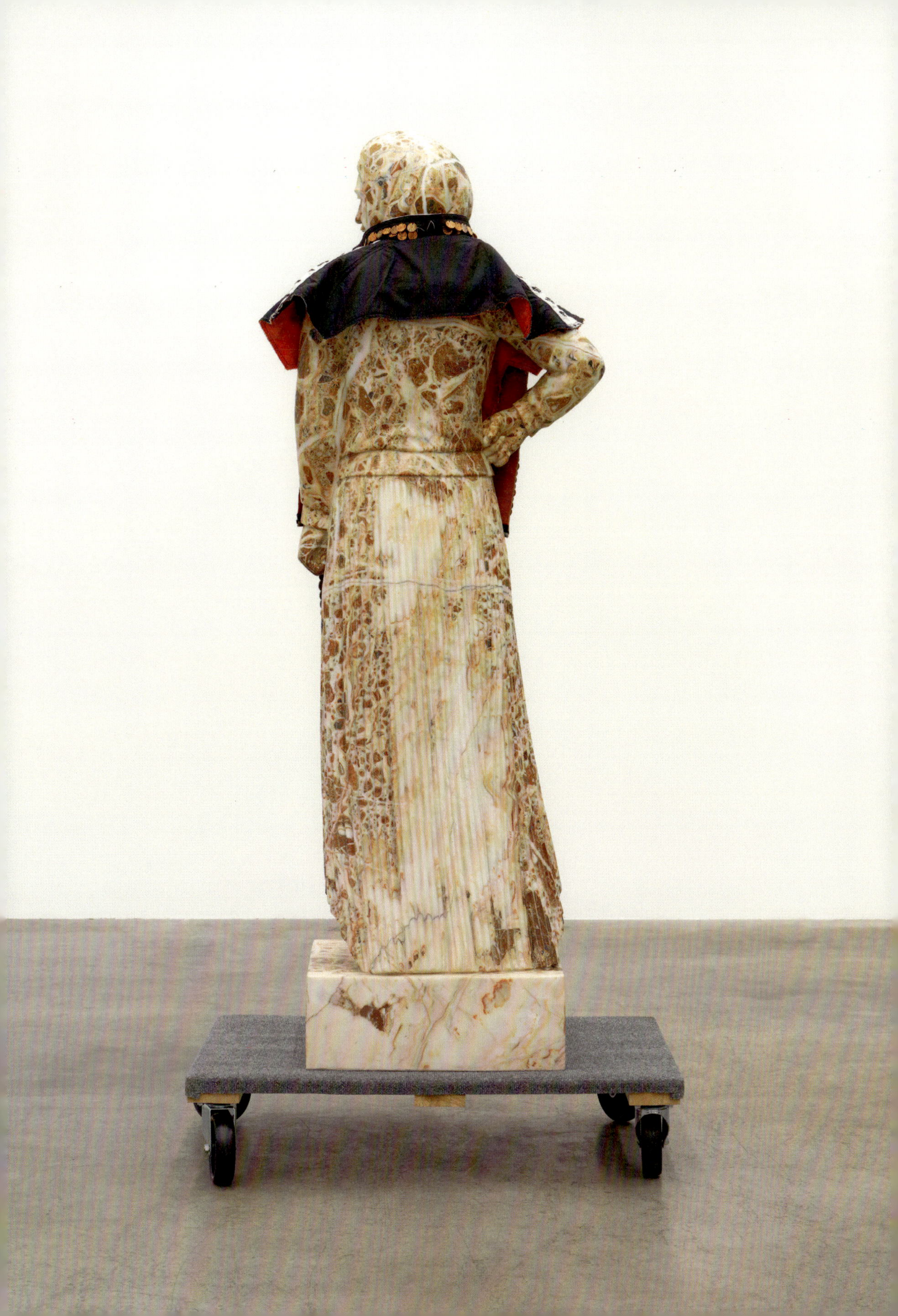

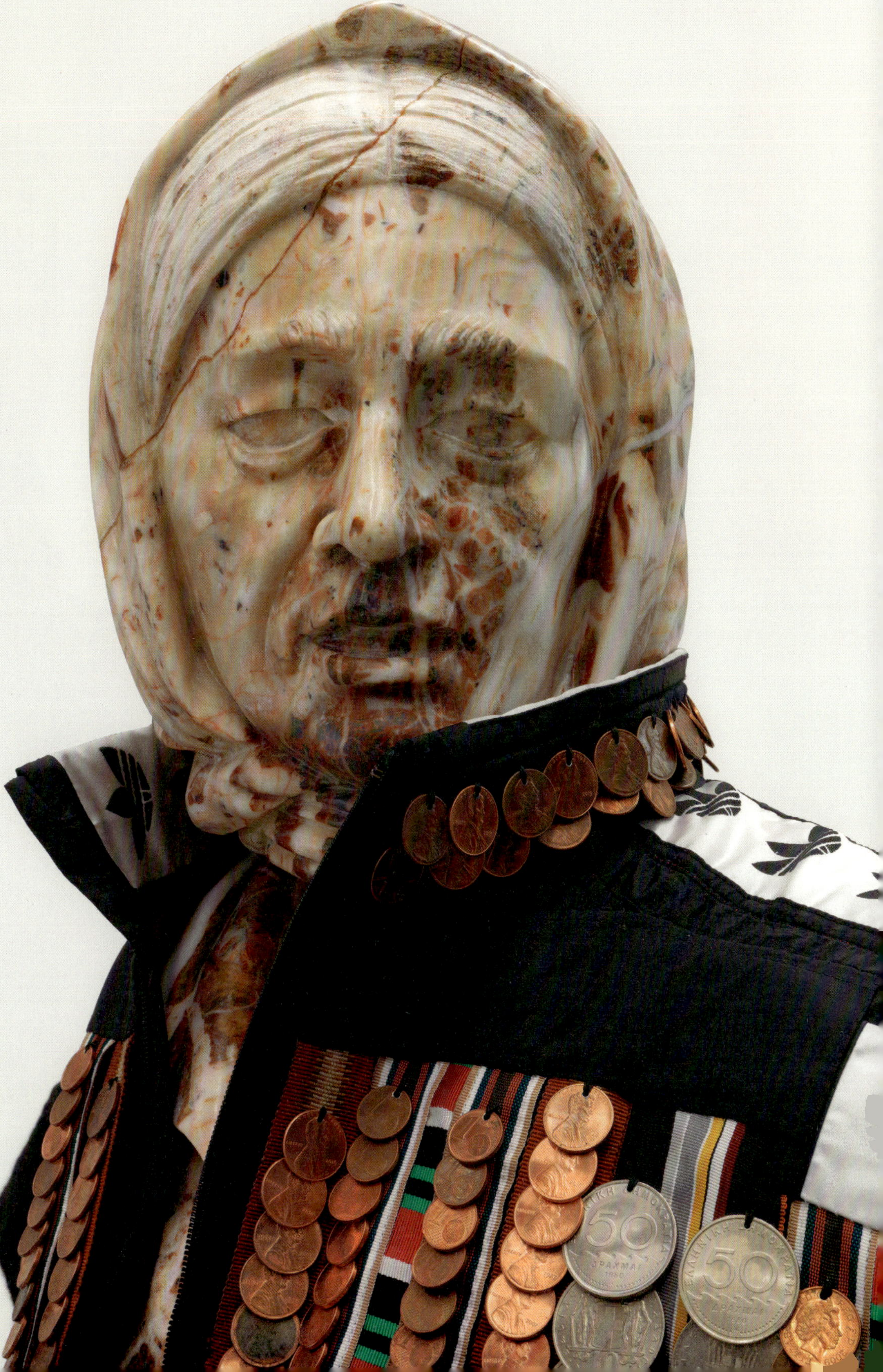

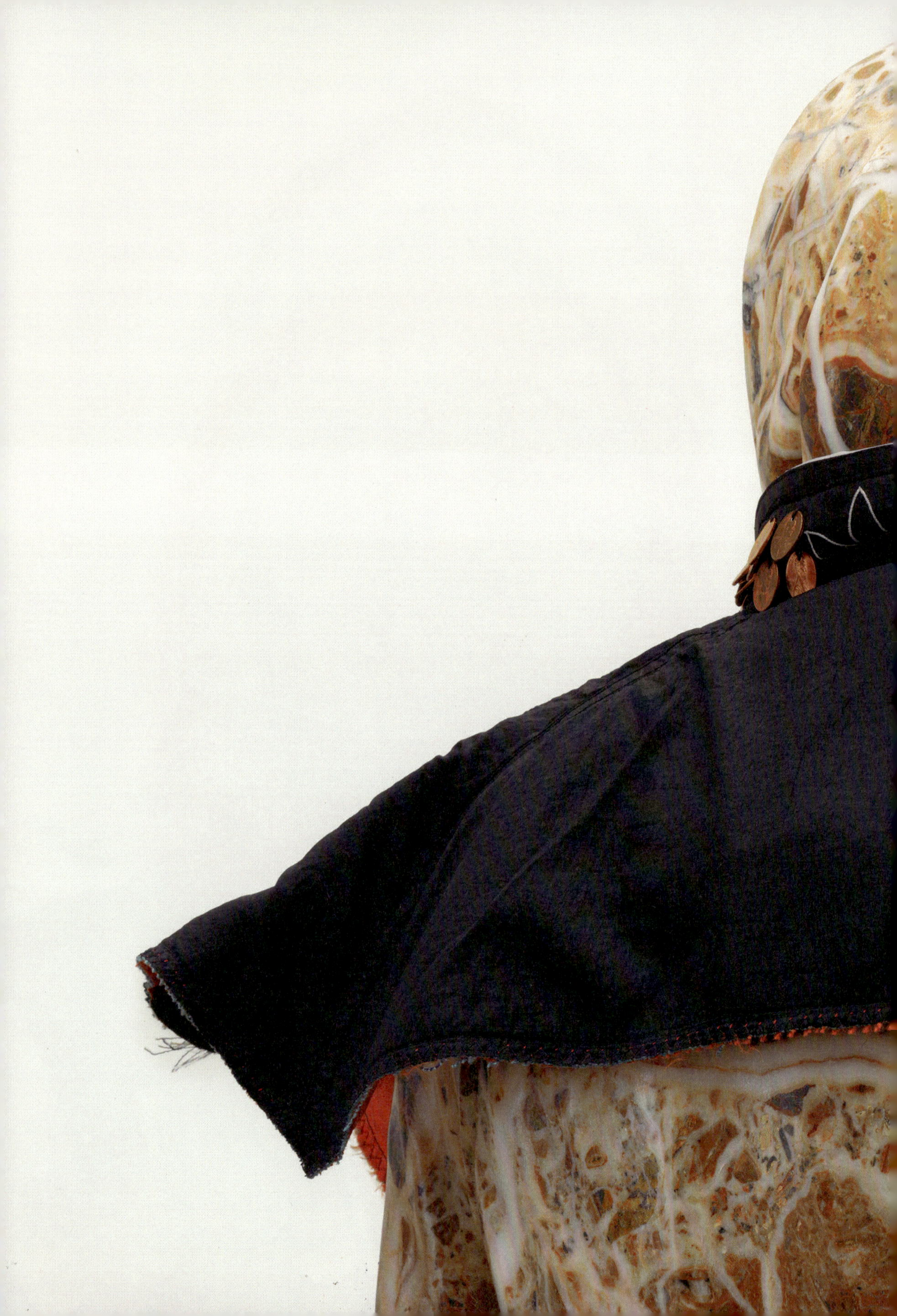

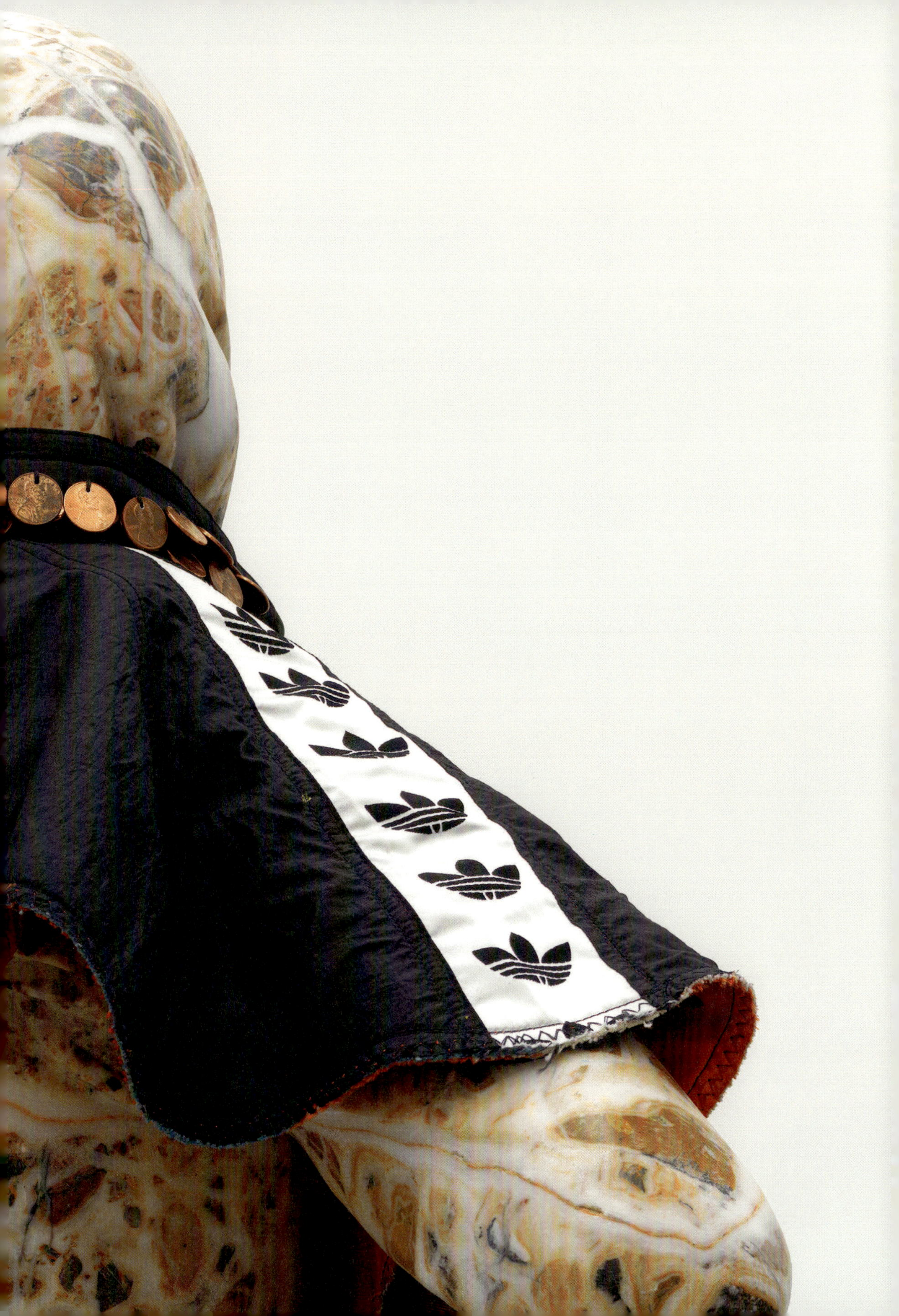

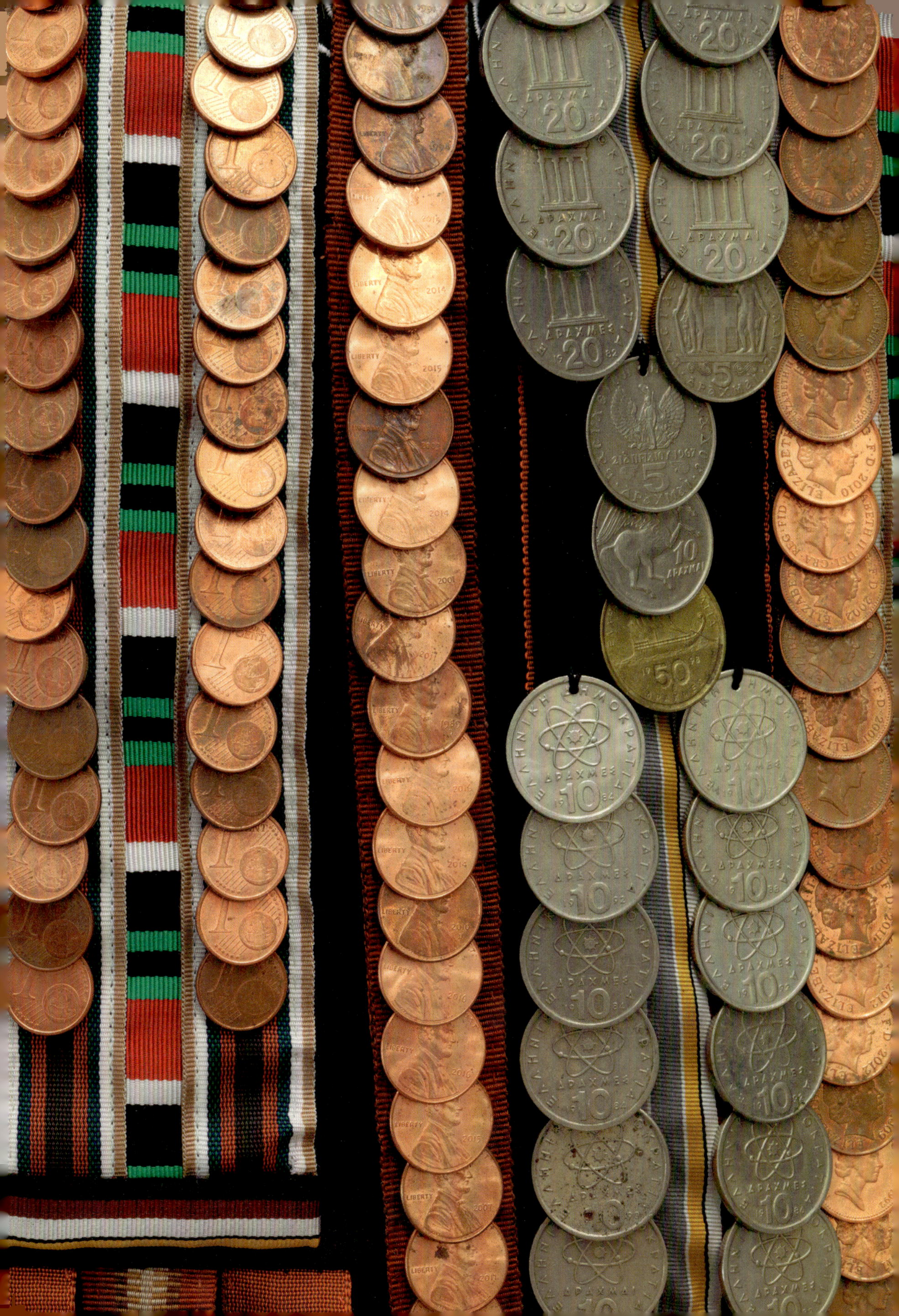

LIST OF WORKS

Floor Licker, 2013
Silicone, wood, metal
195.6 × 7.6 × 10.2 cm

Floor Licker, 2013
Silicone, wood, metal
198 × 7.6 × 10.2 cm

Orthodoctrinator, 2014
Wood and steel beams, wire mesh, urethane foam panels, urethane plastic tiles, wooden seat, fabricated wood, church spires, hair-dryer hoods
300 × 500 × 120 cm

Untitled, 2014
Metal, wood, bicycle seat
100 × 160 × 16 cm

CruciFritz, 2014
Concrete, pigment
64.8 × 63.5 × 17.8 cm

Conversion Table, 2014
Copper, coins, fabric
94 × 46 × 20 cm

Atrophy Room, 2015
Earthenware jugs, Aqua-Resin, paint
Nine parts, dimensions variable
Jug 1: 40.6 × 26.7 × 30.5 cm
Jug 2: 34.3 × 24.1 × 29.2 cm
Jug 3: 24.1 × 28 × 29.2 cm
Jug 4: 22.9 × 18.4 × 30.5 cm
Jug 5: 31.8 × 21.6 × 22.9 cm
Jug 6: 29.8 × 24.1 × 29.2 cm

Jug 7: 30.5 × 20.3 × 35.6 cm
Jug 8: 25.4 × 22.9 × 35.6 cm
Jug 9: 19 × 28 × 30.5 cm

Guarda Che Luna, 2015
Canvas, velvet, plywood panel, Optium, wood frame
185.6 × 199.2 × 10 cm

Slavesitting, 2015
Canvas, velvet, plywood panel, Optium, wood frame
174.5 × 205.5 × 10 cm

Summer Kampf, 2015
Concrete
160 × 68.6 × 20.3 cm

Tomatopig, 2015
Dye on velvet
119.4 × 106.7 cm (framed)

Untitled, 2015
Aqua-Resin, wood, metal
Figure: 121.9 × 54 × 61 cm
Chair: 113 × 61 × 53 cm

Untitled, 2015
Aqua-Resin, wood, urethane plastic
Figure: 101.6 × 35.6 × 33 cm
Chair: 74 × 48 × 51 cm

Commerce Exterieur Mondial Sentimental, 2017
Marble, nylon jacket, gaffer tape, coins, dolly
198 × 45.7 × 61 cm

ARTIST BIO

Andra Ursuța was born in Salonta, Romania, in 1979. She received a BA in art history and visual arts in 2002 from Columbia University, New York. Ursuța documents trauma and tragedy, utilizing a fatalistic dark humor to expose power dynamics, to probe the vulnerability of the human body, and to examine modes of desire. She treats her memories and fears as the inspiration and raw material for her sculptures, drawings, and installations. Mixing media such as cement, plaster, marble, found objects, and wood, her work confronts basic human issues of fear, death, memory, and identity.

Solo exhibitions include *Andra Ursuța: Alps*, New Museum, New York (2016); *Andra Ursuța*, ICA Miami (2015); *Whites*, Kunsthalle Basel (2015); *Hammer Projects: Andra Ursuța*, Hammer Museum, Los Angeles (2014); and *Andra Ursuța*, Palais de Tokyo, Paris (2014). Ursuța has taken part in group exhibitions such as *La Terra Inquieta*, La Triennale di Milano, Milan (2017); *La Grande Madre*, Fondazione Nicola Trussardi at Palazzo Reale, Milan (2015); *Inside*, Palais de Tokyo, Paris (2015); *New Skin*, the Aïshti Foundation, Beirut (2015); *One Torino: SHIT AND DIE*, Palazzo Cavour, Turin (2014); *Body Languages*, Saatchi Gallery, London (2014); *EXPO 1: New York*, MoMA PS1, Long Island City, New York (2013); and *Ostalgia*, New Museum, New York (2012). She participated in the 13th Biennale de Lyon (2015) and the 55th Venice Biennale (2013). Ursuța lives and works in New York City.

AUTHOR BIO

Ali Subotnick is an independent curator and adjunct curator at the Hammer Museum in Los Angeles, where she has organized numerous exhibitions including *UH-OH: Frances Stark 1991–2015* (2015); *The Afghan Carpet Project* (2015); *JG, a film by Tacita Dean* (2013–2014); *LLYN FOULKES* (2013); *Mark Leckey: On Pleasure Bent* (2013); *Made in L.A. 2012* (cocurated with the Hammer's Anne Ellegood and in collaboration with LAXART) and the accompanying Venice Beach Biennial; *Richard Hawkins: Third Mind*, the traveling exhibition originally curated by Lisa Dorin for the Art Institute of Chicago (2011); *The Bible Illuminated: R. Crumb's Book of Genesis* (2010); and *Nine Lives: Visionary Artists from L.A.* (2009). At the Hammer Museum, Subotnick has curated debut American museum exhibitions for artists such as Yuri Ancarani, Neïl Beloufa, Erin Cosgrove, Roberto Cuoghi, Nathalie Djurberg, Julian Hoeber, Jamie Isenstein, Erik van Lieshout, Nathaniel Mellors, Stephen G. Rhodes, and Kaari Upson, as well as Andra Ursuța.

In 2006, along with Maurizio Cattelan and Massimiliano Gioni, she cocurated *Of Mice and Men*, the 4th Berlin Biennale for Contemporary Art. Other collaborations with Cattelan and Gioni include the creation of the Wrong Gallery (2002) and *Charley* magazine (2000). She has written about art and culture for *Frieze*, *Parkett*, *ARTnews*, and *ArtReview*, among other publications, and is the author of *Roberto Cuoghi* and *Kaari Upson*, also in the *2000 Words* series.

When Cecilia Alemani and Massimiliano Gioni brought me to Andra Ursuța's studio in 2014 I immediately connected with her work not only aesthetically but also emotionally. I was amazed by the strikingly bleak humor that is vital to understanding her personal history and identity as a Romanian artist. My sincerest gratitude must go to Andra, who continues to create powerful sculptures, drawings, and installations. Thank you to Ali Subotnick for her excellent writing on Andra's work. I would also like to thank Massimiliano Gioni for both introducing me to Andra and also commissioning all of the essays in this series; Karen Marta and her team at KMEC for their excellent editorial work; and Brendan Dugan, whose design has created an unparalleled visual identity for the *2000 Words* series.

—Dakis Joannou

Andra Ursuța
2000 Words

Commissioning Editor: Massimiliano Gioni
Editor: Karen Marta
Design Concept and Cover: An Art Service
Managing Editor: Tommaso Speretta
Line Editor: Tim Gentles
Project Manager: Regina Alivisatos
Registrar: Natasha Polymeropoulos
Copy Editor: Clare Fentress
Proofreader: Lawrence Levi
Production: The Production Department

Published by:
DESTE Foundation for Contemporary Art
11 Filellinon & Em. Pappa St.
Nea Ionia 142 34
Athens, Greece
www.deste.gr

Available worldwide through:
ARTBOOK | D.A.P.
75 Broad St, Suite 630
New York, NY 10004
www.artbook.com

Available in Greece through:
The DESTE Foundation for Contemporary Art

Printed in Greece by ALTA GRAFICO S.A. Printing and Graphic Arts

ISBN: 978-618-5039-27-1

Pages 21, 23: Photos © Jason Mandella;
Pages 24–25, 27–31: Photos © Annik Wetter;
Pages 32–33: Photo © Uli Holz;
Pages 35, 37: Photos © Fanis Vlastaras & Rebecca Constantopoulou;
Pages 39–47, 49–51, 53, 55: Photos © Todd White Studios;
Pages 57, 59: Photos © Dario Lasagni;
Pages 61, 63, 65, 67, 69–71, 73: Photos © Philipp Hänger;
Pages 75, 77, 79–81, 83: Photos © Alessandro Zambianchi.

Cover: Andra Ursuța, *Conversion Table*, 2014

Thank you to Blaize Lehane at Ramiken Crucible, New York; Ruth Knox, Ellie Nearchou, and Angela Sala at Massimo De Carlo, Milan/London/Hong Kong